In Quest of Spirit

The Bloch Lectures

The Ernest Bloch Professorship of Music and the Ernest Bloch Lectures were established at the University of California in 1962 in order to bring distinguished figures in music to the Berkeley campus from time to time. Made possible by the Jacob and Rosa Stern Musical Fund, the professorship was founded in memory of Ernest Bloch (1880–1959), Professor of Music at Berkeley from 1940 to 1959.

The Ernest Bloch Professors

1964	Ralph Kirkpatrick
1965	Winton Dean
1966	Roger Sessions
1968	Gerald Abraham
1971	Leonard B. Meyer
1972	Edward T. Cone
1975	Donald Jay Grout
1976	Charles Rosen
1977	Alan Tyson
1980	William Malm
1981	Andrew Porter
1982	Ton De Leeuw
1983	James Haar
1985	Richard Crawford
1986	John Blacking
1987	Gunther Schuller
1988	George Perle
1989	László Somfai
1993	Susan McClary
1994	Wye J. Allanbrook
1995	Jonathan Harvey
1997	Lydia Goehr
1998	Izaly I. Zemtsovsky

In Quest of Spirit

Thoughts on Music

Jonathan Harvey

UNIVERSITY OF CALIFORNIA PRESS
BERKELEY   LOS ANGELES   LONDON

University of California Press
Berkeley and Los Angeles, California

University of California Press, Ltd.
London, England

© 1999 by
The Regents of the University of California

Library of Congress Cataloging-in-Publication Data

Harvey, Jonathan, 1939–
     In quest of spirit : thoughts on music / Jonathan Harvey.
          p.   cm. — (Ernest Bloch lectures)
     Includes bibliographical references and index.
     ISBN 0-520-21392-0
     1. Music—Philosophy and aesthetics.   2. Music—Religious aspects.
I. Title.   II. Series.
ML3800.H29   1999
781′.1—DC21   98-19604
                                                                              CIP
                                                                              MN

Printed in the United States of America
9   8   7   6   5   4   3   2   1

The paper used in this publication meets the minimum requirements of
American National Standards for Information Sciences—Permanence of
Paper for Printed Library Materials, ANSI Z39.48-1984.

*The publisher gratefully acknowledges
the generous contribution to this book provided
by The General Endowment Fund of the Associates
of the University of California Press*

Contents

Musical examples follow page 92

CD Excerpts

Preface

This book started out as the Bloch Lectures given at the University of California at Berkeley during a spring semester of almost English wetness in 1995. These lectures, given to a non-specialist public and referring often to well-known examples from the literature, were an attempt to address a subject fairly objectively and musicologically. I was subsequently persuaded that, while transforming them into a book, I should at the same time make them more personal, unashamedly my own subjective viewpoint. The emphasis thus shifted from outer to inner—in the process revealing how this topic, which interested me so much, interwove with my activity as a composer. An important reason for adopting this approach was the apparent impossibility, despite the admitted desirability, of giving definitive answers in a field such as the spirituality of music, probably even for a professional philosopher or theologian. Therefore I rewrote the book as one person's viewpoint, to be taken in conjunction with my own compositional praxis. On the other hand, it would be too easy, it seemed to me, to write an inspiring hymn of praise to the spiritual glories of my favorite composers' scores; that would lead the reader too much, whereas I am happier with a cooler philosophical approach in such an important subject, one that invites the reader to form his or her own knowledge.

The initial spiritual idea, that music was an explanation of the divine universe, has a long and distinguished history. The symmetry of numbers presents itself as both an attractive way to account for an underlying structure in apparently chaotic nature and a fitting way to think of the beauty of God's creative mind; the important idea of music as perceptible numbers, which exemplified this symmetry, thus stretches through history from Pythagoras and his followers to Plato, Boethius, the Corpus Hermeticum, the Camerati, Vincenzo Galilei, Ficino, Fludd, Kircher, Kepler, Newton, and Freemasonry. The writings of Hindemith, Schoenberg, and Stockhausen are not far removed from it either. The idea of music as being essentially entertaining was as alien to such people's attitudes as the idea of philosophy or psychology being essentially entertaining would be today.

Bit by bit the "harmony of the spheres"—the music of the mathematical orderliness of the universe—has receded into mythology as science has encroached, seeming now no more than "random blips and howls picked up by radio telescopes," in the words of Jamie James.[1] The universe has been shown to be infinitely more complex, chaotic, even unknowable than our biblically influenced predecessors thought. It is at best neutral, at worst downright hostile.

Why did intellects of the majesty of Kepler and Newton spend large percentages of their lives thinking about musical intervals and their meaning for science? What did they sense? It was the goal of Unity that attracted them: Unity as sensed in music—precisely measured in numbers by music—and applied to science. Universal laws: simplicity to explain complexity; harmony underlying disorder; universals that really exist (not just as concepts) behind particulars. Unity is an archetype of profound power. It is the most fundamental concept for all mystics, theistic or atheistic. It is the basis of healing, of release from mental suffering, release from the "illusion of self." Someone familiar with the basic truths of Buddhism will have no difficulty seeing where the great *musica mundana* theme has really disappeared—into psychology and into the *sound* of music; that is to say, into music's concept of Harmony (in the broad sense of that word) and into the much-despised *musica instrumentalis* itself. The grand abstraction has been rendered incarnate.

This book attempts to tackle such big issues in the belief that it is important that we become more conscious: conscious of who we are and what is important to us. It is particularly important at the present critical time, when the available scientific power is so ambiguous. It is hard to say anything along these lines without appearing banal or ignorant. The big questions of existence generally are thought to lie outside the normal domain of science. In art, meanwhile, the complexity of the world is all too often taken to be most faithfully represented by mystification: a sense of chaos, of untraceable meaning, is thought to be more congruent with how things are, with the perceived breakdown of structures—moral, social, cultural, philosophical, scientific, religious, economical, ecological. Much twentieth-century art has practiced, and practices still, something close to mystification.

Yet is there not something evasive about the perpetual hovering in the darkness of the unconscious, lit only by strange feelings of fear, nameless desire, alienation in a baffling world? For art to address a big question such as the nature of mystical experience is frequently dismissed as pretentiously inadmissible in the context of both the threatening forces of the universe and postmodern culture. The horror underlying existence in our time is that we no longer believe the true to be the good; it is now the indifferent, or the horrific, or merely the hopelessly inaccessible. (How different a time from that of the Newtonian Mozart, basking in the warmth of the Enlightenment!) It may well be salutary that the focus is now more on the ontological, on how it is to be, than on the epistemological, the attempt to know. Although it is an entirely acceptable prospect that the art of today and tomorrow must be plausibly complex in a reason-defying way, drawing largely on mysterious

intuitions, let us not harbor false hopes. Chance or semiran-
dom procedures or obscurity should not be used as a dishon-
est surface to cover vacuousness or to dissemble the illusion of
elite knowledge; rather, let these processes reflect fullness more
adequately. Some art seems to say to its audience: "I don't
know, but I'm defiantly putting on a dazzling show anyway—
and you won't understand it either." For me, great art tries a bit
harder for truth, whatever the odds.

I cannot conceive of spending my life in a heedlessly uneth-
ical pursuit. Composing is a part of trying to live a life "skill-
fully," as Buddhists say. One can compose from many different
levels of the soul, base or elevated; the decision is important. I
do not believe in composing for a worse future, promoting
divisive, egotistical forces, or choosing a pessimistic aesthetic
(the choice of mind-set is surprisingly free). I would rather be
silent. I aspire to a future in which the deepest level of personality known to human beings, the radiant, still point beyond
words, is encouraged by music to become manifest. Such a
point will contain it all (the worst too), yet if we can find again
the value of these words, it will be both *true* and *good*.

Acknowledgments

To be invited to Berkeley as 1995 Bloch Lecturer was both a privilege and a pleasure. I would like to thank those who arranged for my stay and made it so enjoyable, particularly Richard Feliciano, David Wessel, and Olly Wilson. Once the lectures were turned into book form they were scrutinized by Terry Diffey, Arthur Low, and Peter Abbs, from whom I received extremely helpful comments. I would like to thank them all. Also I received the invaluable relief of Norm Sacuta's typing of my manuscript, so composing did not have to be abandoned for too long. I am most grateful to Clive Williamson for recording the Scriabin excerpt for me, especially welcome in view of the horrendous complications and expenses involved in trying to get permission to include excerpts from commercial recordings, an enterprise that proved for the most part impossible. For help making the "master" for the CD included in this book I am most grateful to Juan Pampin at Stanford University and Colin Attwell at Claudio Records. At the University of California Press, Doris Kretschmer, Juliane Brand, and Lynne Withey helped things along, despite many obstacles, patiently and charmingly. Anne G. Canright was a magnificent editor, clarifying the sense and improving the flow throughout. Thank you to all.

1

Who Is the Composer?

The purpose of this book is to describe a journey, not particularly or necessarily my journey, but one in which many share.
A brief outline of my own spiritual experience, however,
should provide a perspective in which the thoughts and opin-
ions offered here may be placed; for such a subject as music's
connection with spirituality is bound to be more subjective,
less objective, than many. In an important sense, in fact, a
dualistic subject/object distinction is inappropriate when deal-
ing with music. For music is intimately concerned with transcending that dichotomy, with healing Descartes's ontological
separation of self and world and Kant's epistemological separation of self and certain knowledge, both formative of today's
dominant paradigms (and difficulties).

My spiritual journey started, as journeys often do, in a kind
of womb—that of the church. When I was nine my parents sent
me off to be a chorister at St. Michael's College, Tenbury, in the
heart of the Worcestershire countryside. The school was
founded in the nineteenth century by Sir Frederick Arthur Gore
Ousley (we always pronounced the complete name) to foster the
revival of music in the Church of England. Ousley was a professor at Oxford, a composer of church music, and a noted col-
lector of books and manuscripts. At St. Michael's I often gazed

at the *Messiah* score Handel used for its Dublin performance. Then I could touch the sacred paper; now it is kept behind several inches of metal and many locks. Alone in the beautiful library I spent hours taking off the shelves the various tomes of sweet-smelling old music and trying to play it on the piano, absconding from walks and more healthy-minded school activities for as long as I was undiscovered. The magic of those hours—seeing everything for the first time—was intense.

But sweetest of all were the hours spent singing Matins and Evensong every day in the colorful Victorian chapel. Scarcely anyone was there but us. Our solitary reverence was not unrelieved, however. I can remember the obsessive games of Bible cricket played with my neighbors in the heavy choir stalls during the reading of the lessons. We would take a passage from Scripture and decode it into score sheets: a = a single, b = bowled, c = caught, d = 2, e = 3, f = a boundary, and so on to l = leg-before-wicket and beyond.

Nevertheless, the glory of singing to nobody but God, the sunlight streaming through the stained glass, was part of the same world of childish excitement. At times we would attain an epiphanic splendor—in a Lassus motet, in a recent canticle, using the full power of the large Father Willis organ. I would get the key and enter the church, often after dark, to play strange improvisations on this organ. The silence of the building was haunting, very frightening—yet I was fascinated. Why? I don't know. Music came out of it, dissolved back into it. There were ghosts.

The main discovery of the next years, those of adolescence, was nature. I loved to be alone in its presence and would cycle off at dusk to Sutton Park, a stretch of some six square miles of heathland woods and lakes, to wander in the half-light. I discovered that I only had to hold my breath, metaphorically, and look and listen, and "it" would happen: a mysterious sensation of *longing* would overcome me—as if I was perceiving some sacred thing—quite indefinable—of infinite delight, tasted but not possessed. It seemed common then; now I have more understanding, and it is less common.

Although I questioned Christianity and became an atheist in

my teens, the potential for mystical experience never left. In 1960, as a Cambridge student browsing in a bookshop, I came across Evelyn Underhill's *Mysticism*. This book changed my life. It gave form to all the vague yearnings I had experienced. I found myself recognizing the things she wrote about, confirming outside myself what was half formed within. From then on I had the support to continue listening to the small voice that whispered sweetly and secretly. It is fatally easy to dismiss that delicate message, because it does not square with the worldview of society, friends, or teachers. Science told me nothing of it, empiricism and reason even less. Yet it is everything: the heart, the source, of all the rest. That was the conviction Underhill gave me. I had found I was not alone, but part of a substantial tradition. Around that time every evening I would spend maybe an hour in the darkened Catholic church in Cambridge gazing at the sanctuary light, quite still. It was the church Rosa, my wife, and I were married in.

My love of the Christian mystics produced fruit in several compositions, notably *Ludus Amoris* (1969). Here the fierce ardor of the Spanish mystical tradition (St. John of the Cross, Diego de Estella, Juan de los Angeles, Ramón Lull, Francisco de Osuna) provided a healing resolution in light and love of the conflicts expressed by David Gascoyne's harrowing *De Profundis* and *Inferno* and George Seferis's mythically resonant but nihilistic poetry ("They told us, you will conquer when you submit. / We submitted and found dust and ashes"). There was even a sixties-style agit-prop demonstration in the score, which, incidentally, I gather Edward Heath (our former prime minister) in the audience found quite intolerable. Nevertheless, despite all its raw faults, the mystical embrace of the resolution hit a nerve: it became the first work in the 245-year history of the Three Choirs Festival to be applauded in a cathedral. The title referred to the game of love, more like a game of hide-and-seek, that God plays with us—now absent, now intense beyond belief.

My mother had just died when I came to write the work. Whether because of her inherent goodness or her firm Christian faith, her death was a profound rite of passage for me.

Although her last illness was long and debilitating, the love expressed in her eyes, the way she spoke and looked at me in those weeks, was so extraordinary, so beyond anything that had come before, that I could not doubt that I had witnessed in her some new stage of realization or enlightenment at the gate of death. Since then death has seemed to me a key with which to unlock life: awkward, a nagging misfit in our scheme of consciousness, yet capable of taking our understanding much higher, if we allow it.

A little later I encountered, on a friend's recommendation, Rudolf Steiner's books and lectures—I read forty or fifty volumes, such was my fascination. Steiner saw death simply as a gateway, not particularly important in its own right, but one of many. He was a Hegelian philosopher, a scientist, and an artist—and also a seer, a clairvoyant. He claimed to decipher (from direct vision) what happens after death, between death and a rebirth, and during birth and death themselves. He discerned the subtle light-filled radiance of those intermediate worlds and other "higher" worlds and described them almost in the language of art; in fact, his view of art, and in particular of music, was that it is the communicating link between levels of perception, spiritual and material, clairvoyant and normal. He made a world of delicate light come alive to my imagination, a sphere too refined for normal perception yet accessible to meditation and higher imagination—a participatory epistemology beyond the Kantian closure—in which the self and nature are inseparable: one unified interdependency.

My thinking was certainly taking clearer form with such guides as Steiner. Yet for all his emphasis on meditation, I could not practice it regularly; the aim was not sufficiently crisply defined. In 1977 I encountered Hindu, or rather Vedic, meditation practice in the form of transcendental meditation. This effective and simple practice, coupled with the Sidhi sutras of Patanjali, gave a philosophy of experience, a liberation from the Western paradigm that philosophy can be sorted out by clear thinking alone. Vedic thought, though highly complex, can be understood only by experiencing deeper states of consciousness. These were mapped out in the teachings, together with lucid signposts to help one orient oneself. Somehow that year for the first time I got into the habit of meditating twice daily, and have never lapsed for more than a day or two.

Maharishi Mahesh Yogi, the founder of this school of revived ancient meditation, is predominantly a *bhakti* yogi, that is to say, a man of devotion and love. His influence was pervasive in *Bhakti* (1982), which I conceived largely on a retreat to learn the Sidhis; each movement quotes a passage from a Vedic hymn. It is also present in *The Path of Devotion* (1983), which used some of his words. In this work the texts progress from expressions of homely, simple love to an image of a drop of water becoming lost in the ocean and other metaphors of loss of self in all-love. Works like *Madonna of Winter and Spring* (1986) were influenced by the quasi-archetypal form of a typical meditation. One leaves the tumult of a busy day to settle the mind until it reaches a point of quiescence. There it stays for a while, empty. From that level new, radiant, and often blissful thoughts and feelings arise. Several works, for instance String Quartet no. 1 and *From Silence* (1988), start with an invocation to emptiness by sounding a "zero-sound"—a long, almost featureless note or complex. This does the opposite of most openings, which seek to arouse, to excite the listener's interest. Instead, the aim is to invite the listener to a quieter level, there to attend with a subtler, "more refined," more delicate perception, as Vedic philosophy maintains.

Finally (so far—for nothing is predictable or conclusive on this journey), I came to want a greater synthesis between my reason and my nagging questioning of the inherent existence of God or gods. Having spent so much of my life in universities, I was fully aware of the force of scientific empiricism and also of scientific uncertainty; of the relative, perspectival nature of "facts"; of postmodernism in all its forms. To me, the most profound way of thinking that reconciled such nihilistic views with my spiritual certainties was Buddhist. When encountered superficially, Buddhism, with its doctrine of emptiness, the idea that nothing, not even oneself, has inherent existence outside self-grasping delusion, can seem quite nihilistic. In fact, however, it embraced much of what is now current in critical theory, Derrida, and Lacan millennia ago, emerging as a blissfully happy and fulfilling, compassionate and ethical, way of life.

Perhaps it is a legacy of my love of sacred figures and their personalities that I prefer Tibetan Mahayana Buddhism to other forms, although Zen has immense value to me as well. Tibetan Buddhism not only has many "saints," bodhisattvas, and buddhas—it is quite personalized—but it also places a strong emphasis on ethics. At one time in my life I often visited Christian monasteries, and I was greatly inspired by the look I would sometimes see in the faces of the contemplatives, a look telling, more than anything else I encountered in life or books, about truth and values. Selfless Christian love leading to profound peace I find again in Buddhism, as I do in Vedic and Anthroposophical experience of higher consciousness. There is no question of eliminating earlier spiritual selves, only of incorporating them. The connecting thread is the music I write: I guide the music, and it guides me (it often seems to come through me semiautonomously). This double process defines the religion of a composer, I suppose; it is always a quest, for music and through music. There should be no divisions between journey and traveler, or between journey and goal.

My aim in this book, then, is to explore the two things that concern me most—music and spirituality—in the sphere where they overlap. This sphere is a large one for some people, a small one for others, and many will disagree as to what falls into it. It seems, in the end, to be a subjective matter of taste. Even when music sets a sacred or spiritual text, or is illustrative of one, there is no guarantee of a consensus as to its nature. I would find it perfectly natural, for instance, for someone to judge Verdi's *Requiem* as not a spiritual mass at all. And whereas the nineteenth-century musician Franz Xaver Witt (he founded the Universal German Cecilia Association in

1867), for instance, seized on Mozart's later use of parts of the *Coronation* Mass in operas to castigate the "sheer immoralities" of his masses,[1] Karl Barth wrote of that same church music that "it evidently comes from on high," and the theologian Hans Kung found in them "traces of transcendence."[2]

Not only might the category "spiritual" be said to be subjective, it might also be said to be excessively broad. Benjamin Britten, though not obviously a religious man, once remarked that he thought of all of his music as glorifying God. Those of firm religious conviction have no trouble including their composing activity in the same sphere as their spiritual life, their life of worship: the continuity is clear. *"Soli Deo Gloria,"* as Haydn humbly wrote at the end of several of his scores.

If the spiritual in music is so subjective and so broad, how on earth can we isolate it for discussion? One way might be to define what music is *not* spiritual, and why not. Or if we take the view that music is by its very nature spiritual—a prevalent view, in one form or another, throughout history—we must determine if there are degrees of intensity to unpack within the word *spiritual*. Perhaps the property is manifested more or less powerfully. Philosophy since Wittgenstein's discussion of "games" has tended to view the spiritual as a cluster of properties rather than a single all-encompassing one. We may even find that "spirituality" is not quite the term we are looking for. It is not a comfortable word, somehow. In addition, of course, we need to try to determine what music's nature is and how it differs from other things. In what follows we will examine the question of "subjective taste," and I will show that it is at the root of what music is about: the very thing that makes our discussion so cumbersome, the relationship of word to world, is what music gloriously resolves.

As an example of a work that is *not* spiritual, I would like to propose a piece of my own called *The Riot*. In explaining why I choose that piece to illustrate the category, I hope that the dividing line between spiritual and nonspiritual will become clearer.

A preliminary caveat, though: you are certainly free to disagree with a composer's view of his own work. The artist's

intention in creating a piece is not necessarily the most important ingredient in your apprehension of it. One distinguished
professor of music in England, for example, wrote: "Even the
most secular elements in his music acquire a radiance that can
only be felt as contained within a mystical experience; and that
is my reaction even to *The Riot*, which for me, at least, has an
underlying and unifying meditative quality (a joyful meditation certainly) not disturbed by the surface dislocations."[3]

So why do I find *The Riot* nonspiritual? I suppose most of us
would be inclined to use the word *spiritual* to describe works
that we feel are profound, that touch us at some very deep,
very important, level. Works to which we apply such adjectives
as *playful, ingenious, witty,* and *lightweight* we would not call
spiritual.

A lofty, *ethical* tone is not necessarily required to qualify for
the spiritual category either. *L'incoronazione di Poppea* by
Monteverdi and Berg's *Lulu* are both ethically suspect, representing on stage the triumph of evil and the reign of pessimism, respectively. Yet if we respond deeply to the music,
both stories are somehow transfigured *by* the music, which
seems to make the subject matter reach beyond itself to some
other, more reconciled level; in the latter case especially, the
ultimate effect is to provide a liberating insight into the essential nature of human suffering.

Perhaps the category of the spiritual, then, is demarcated by
the feeling we have of the music having somehow reached
beyond, rather than by any associations evoked by a text, "program," or the composer's stated intention. We shall return to
these ideas later.

Meanwhile, let me explain why I call *The Riot* predominantly
nonspiritual. It was commissioned by Het Trio, an energetic
and high-spirited group—flute, bass clarinet, and piano—from
Amsterdam specializing in tough, often punchy, avant-garde
music. The title is an anagram of Het Trio ("The Trio" in Dutch)
and points to a riot of color, energy, and high jinks. The middle
section is based on jazz piano virtuosity, and later everybody
plays in swing mode with boogie-woogie undertones. There is

also a crazy use of a classical cycle-of-fifths sequence. The whole thing is just a little over the top.

This is the opening:

CD 1: *The Riot*

And here is the recapitulation of material in swing mode:

CD 2: *The Riot*

Occurring in between, here is how the jazz style breaks out, and how it leads to the circle of fifths:

CD 3: *The Riot*

You now know my intentions and your own reactions to this music, which may, for the moment at least, have decided you as to whether spirituality is present or not. The overriding factor in such a decision is the nature of your response, your state of mind when experiencing the sounds. We may clearly recognize when we feel ourselves to be in a spiritual, or some other, state. Equally clearly, we may experience a similar state of consciousness every time we hear certain music and so impute a given quality to the music based on the reaction that it always arouses.

The strength of this link between music and meaning can be questioned from at least two points of view, though not, I think, in a fundamentally damaging way.

The first can be illustrated by a typically Romantic view of meaning expressed by Louis Spohr, who noted in his autobiography: "Jean Paul appeared to interest himself very much for this new composition [the String Quartet op. 45, no. 1] and ascribed to it a highly poetic signification, of which while composing I certainly never thought, but which recurred in a very striking manner to my mind at every subsequent performance of the quartet."[4]

Here two things are stuck together by association, and they are subsequently very difficult to unstick. Stravinsky sternly corrected this sort of reaction in a famous early statement: "If . . . music appears to express something, this is only an illusion

and not a reality. It is simply an additional attribute which . . .
we have lent it, thrust upon it, as a label, a convention—in
short, an aspect, unconsciously or by force of habit, we have
come to confuse with its essential being."[5] Even so, surely the
"essential being" to which Stravinsky refers is strictly speaking
a far-from-innocent concept; most people's experience is probably quite as lacking in innocence as was Spohr's.

The second point of view concerns a more powerful meaning of the spiritual, which we might call (fashionably) a "peak
experience." Such moments are notoriously capricious and
unpredictable, in music as in life, and many will object that we
never know where and by what we will be transported.

In a world that is in a constant state of flux, it is our nature
to create consistency, and therefore we categorize: Bach's B
Minor Mass is a spiritual work. There is a consensus that
makes such a belief broadly true, but we also know that we
may at any performance find it untrue. Equally, we may be
unexpectedly enraptured by some quite "trivial" pop or folk
song that somehow opens an inner door. Our spiritual label-
ing, in other words, can be unreliable.

Talking of *The Riot* raises another question, a central one
since roughly the time of Mallarmé, that strikes at the very heart
of meaning. Much of the work of critical theory has been concerned with deconstructing the author's or composer's voice,
with establishing just how utterances, ever shifting, ever deriv-
ative, in fact depend on historical musical systems, instruments, economic circumstances, social conditioning, codes
of understanding, and so on. Clearly, one might conclude, all
authors are shoplifters: they take and ingest what's around.
They are themselves "shifting complexes" constituted by the
times in which they live. This is a valuable truth, but it leaves
important factors out.

An essentialist and intuitive reaction to such a criticism
might be that it applies even to how we view our friends. Yet
we know them as highly distinctive, precious beings, unique
and special to us. We even feel it with a friend we have not seen

for thirty years. Indeed, if we have forgotten everything else about someone, there often remains to our recollection a faint but still distinctively unified essence. We find the same two-sidedness in works of music. At first, before we know anything of a composer's other work, we may hear only fragmented references, flying centrifugally off into the society and musical realm that make the composer's constituting context. (The history of new music criticism is littered with the corpses of reviews that fail to hear anything but the references.) Then, as we get to hear more works, and the same works more often, we may begin to develop a sense of friendship. We experience not fragments, but a complex, unified voice we "know" in an almost I-thou relationship. The movement is now centripetal. This has been my experience, at least, with every composer I love (and to use that word, as most of us do about composers, clinches the point—it is a knowledge involving love). Nevertheless, despite these profound feelings, we must ask ourselves whether we are not attaching ourselves to a personality that we have ourselves created, conceptualized, and projected. I leave this disturbing question open for the moment.

The deconstruction issue might now be illustrated by revealing what lurked in my mind, as far as I can remember, when I composed *The Riot*. Of course, it must be pointed out that it can take five to ten minutes to compose a single chord, and literally hundreds of thoughts cross one's mind during the period of that chord's genesis: memories of similar sounds in many other pieces; associations of those sounds with people, dramas, sensations. Clearly there is little chance of one's mind being so blank as to allow one to compose so-called abstract music, which is just itself and nothing else; the mind is too active.

However, I can point here to the main associative backdrops to *The Riot*. (Composers don't normally like to do this because they feel it diminishes a piece's originality. It even threatens one's precious egotistical sense of self. These concerns are real enough, though they could be answered with the assertion that, as with the notion of "friend," originality exists at another transcendent level and cannot be compromised by such inner revelations and confessions.)

The opening was to have a formal, ritualistic feel, and what came to my mind can in a sense be heard "via" Stravinsky's *Symphonies of Wind Instruments* (see example 1). Many people also hear this piece "via" Russian folk music, notably those somewhat acquainted with that genre. So here we have at least three levels of listening: three composers are at work—Harvey, Stravinsky, and an anonymous folk singer.

CD 4: *The Riot*

The second idea grew from a passage in a trio by the Dutch composer Jan Rokus van Roosendaal—one of some dozen recordings made by Het Trio of works previously written for them, which they sent me, presumably to help my thinking. The passage has a repetitive rhythm, derived, the composer writes in his notes, from Indian rhythmic techniques (he studied the tabla for several years). So here again there are at least three levels of authorship: Indian music, van Roosendaal, Harvey.

First, the van Roosendaal passage:

CD 5: *Kaida*

Then, *The Riot:*

CD 6: *The Riot*

The third theme derives from vague memories of oriental piping and the fierce, raucous, obsessive sounds of certain Indian oboe recordings. I used the same model before in my *Ritual Melodies* for tape (1990); here is one of the computer-simulated melodies from that work:

CD 7: *Ritual Melodies*

And here is the new working of *The Riot*. It is played by the bass clarinet, while the piano accompaniment has the Indian rhythm idea:

CD 8: *The Riot*

The fourth theme derives from Scriabin, a composer whose fluid rhythms and original harmonies and textures, particularly in the late sonatas, have always bewitched me; I even admire, with some reservations, the mystical tone. He was a favorite of my father's, and so I heard much Scriabin from my first years on.

Here is a passage from the Sonata no. 10:

CD 9: Scriabin, Sonata no. 10

The theme in *The Riot* comes in the piano underneath the Stravinsky and Indian oboe ideas and eventually takes over:

CD 10: *The Riot*

I thought of this music also as representing the feminine side of my nature, in contrast to the macho music around it. And I saw a connection with the French tradition leading to Boulez (who loves late Scriabin) and beyond.

Another idea was suggested by a colleague, David Osmond-Smith, when he heard me say I didn't know what to write for this commission. He suggested, "Why not just put some notes in a hat and pull them out?" I know that under his quirky sense of humor he has a serious propensity for the irrational and anarchic, as seen also in the aesthetics of Berio and the younger Italian avant-gardists, so, although I laughed, my mind secretly and seriously ticked away—I couldn't get rid of this absurd idea. Sure enough, I eventually found precisely the brief element of chaos needed to be dropped in at certain points: it had the function of articulation—leavening the careful thematic working like a fool in a Shakespeare play. A high-spirited work should allow anarchy; what is humor if not an irruption of disorder? Here is one such passage:

CD 11: *The Riot*

In these examples we see how chance encounters with music or a timely casual remark can trigger a thought process that gathers together impulses already present in unconscious memory, impulses of feeling and form.

The circle-of-fifths idea derived from the fact that I was teaching Mozart piano concertos to students at that moment. This allied itself to a wonderful sensation of vertigo that I experience when a composer goes several steps in this cycle, preferably without inserting the diminished fifth necessary to keep it diatonic; in other words, the progressions go over the top and fly free of tonality, although the surface of the music is still tonal. It's a kind of classical atonality.

Also, I was pushed in the same direction by the first theme, the Stravinsky-like one, which, with its pentatonicism, highlighted fourths, fifths, and minor sevenths, led me to the fourths and fifths of the bass in the circle of fifths (see example 2). The jazz idea is dominated by one of the same intervals, the minor seventh, deriving from the same semiconscious impulse, the first theme's intervallicism, and these also move atonally—in chromatic scales (see example 3). An example of the sort of thing I mean is Mozart's C Minor Concerto, K. 491, first movement development section (see example 4). And here's the result—not a close relationship, really just a transference of principle:

CD 12: *The Riot*

To track down every source would be tedious; the jazz ones, for instance, are obvious enough. But I'll finally mention a technique that is becoming increasingly significant in music of our time, one deriving from electronic music, and that is the very simple device of multispeed delay. A sound is fed into the processor, which then replays it, diminuendoing at two or more different speeds, like an echo bounding around in different acoustic spaces. I heard a striking use of this cliché of the studio in an orchestral work, *Seuils* by Marc-André Dalbavie, a young French composer I have often met at IRCAM (Institut de Recherche et Coordination Acoustique/Musique), and it told me how interesting such a device could be when not done by a machine, but by instrumentalists with all their unmechanical inexactnesses.

CD 13: *The Riot*

This, then, became my main strategy for draining away the energies—a sudden emptying of invention, a return to rest. I used it at key points, and most of all at the end.

So, having somewhat deconstructed my own work, I can ask who, finally, is the composer? Pretty well every note derives from one or many other sources. Even the structural coherence, by which I mean the way in which subcutaneous intervallic complexes of time and pitch are repeated over and over again, is in no sense my own idea: it was taught me by teachers, study, and experience.

Yet my friends and those who know my work say I have a distinctive voice. What, if it exists, does it consist of? Are they imagining an illusion—an illusion similar to that which Roland Barthes describes as the death of the author, or that which Buddhists refer to as the illusion of personality? We talk ourselves into an "as-if" heuristic personality, an ego patched together out of scraps and fragments, ultimately unimportant; but we persuade others to take it seriously. Is it the elusive "subject" of psycholinguistics, the ever-fluctuating personality that clearly exists only in terms of the language in which its personality operates? Should we not perhaps exalt honestly the polyphonic, many-voiced personalities we really are?

I raise these questions not to answer them now (they are enormous) but to show that deconstruction is a way of trying to see what music and its expression are; it is a perspective quite different from traditional textbook theory, but now very important. From this standpoint, we may begin the slow journey to an understanding of what "spirituality in music," such a natural concept for composers of the past, might mean today.

The Riot, then, is not much of a spiritual work from two points of view: It is composed of other music (how can borrowed music be an expression of the innermost soul?). This objection invokes a Romantic idea of creativity, one that would not be held by Bach or Handel, for instance, who "borrowed" for their sacred works fairly liberally. Also, it is concerned with playfulness and humor to a considerable degree.

However, even this simple statement is ambiguous. *The Riot* may not be only other music, for one thing; also, it seems to hint at, or even reveal, to some listeners who know me as a musical friend, a level pointing toward transcendence: surely a spiritual quality. (What "transcendence" means we must return to.) Of course, I chose here to examine *The Riot* because I find its dissection less painful, less revealing, than that of a work closer to my heart. The "heart" or spiritual center is something I protectively sense in myself—whether truly or falsely, we will have to see.

Let us consider another work that is aware of its own derivativeness: Stravinsky's *The Rake's Progress.* Scarcely any recent composer can have been so averse to revealing authorial self-expression: Stravinsky found personal emotion repulsive in unmediated form, as occurs in the case of Wagner or (his mother's favorite, interestingly enough) Scriabin. After the period of *The Rite of Spring* (1913), the violent appearance of *Pulcinella* (1920) is almost unparalleled in the history of music: in it, a sudden hiding takes place, a total renunciation of fashionable modernism, as Stravinsky resorts to playing around in place of striving forward.

At the other end of the neoclassical period, *The Rake's Progress* of 1951 is the most explicit manifestation of self-effacement of all. And many people, myself included, find it a curiously moving and spiritual work. Ingmar Bergman, with Stravinsky's apparent approval, was the first to imply links between the chastened Tom Rakewell and Christ—not something one can do with very many opera heroes. On the surface, however, it is a fast-moving Mozartean comedy full of wit and theatrical conceits—out-and-out conventions and contrivances. Many of the musical derivations are Mozartean as well, with the odd bel canto Italian reference heard now and then. The point seems to be to make transparent the creative process and its essentially kleptomaniacal nature—and then to have witty play with it. Meaning comes not from authorship, but from formal pattern-play and ingenuity.

This is partly a result of linking arms with Mozart and Donizetti, composers who were hardly invited in for heavy messages. Perhaps Mozart lies too deep and Donizetti too shallow.

The feel of Stravinsky's pastiche is that each self-contained number in turn is a musical performance, even a *singer's* performance, appropriate to the action of the moment but not actually expressive of it.

When we reach the end, however, the models change. Nick Shadow, the devil to whom Tom has capitulated by allowing himself to be given a life of empty luxury, finally fails to claim his "wages," Tom's soul, because at the crucial moment Tom remembers Ann, his pure and innocent beloved. But Tom has only a partial triumph. Shadow, Tom's dark side in a sense, is now injected directly into Tom's mind, which, unable to take the strain, collapses into insanity. Thus, instead of Shadow taking Tom to hell, Tom takes Shadow into himself and lives on, though fatally wounded. To mirror these events, the models for the music become increasingly baroque. Not only baroque dance forms but also Bachian Passion forms appear. It's as if the weighty cadences of the high baroque are called on to seal the climax of the opera, without betraying the principle of authorial absence.

An example is "Am Abend da es kühle war" from the *St. Matthew Passion,* which I think may have been the sort of memory in Stravinsky's mind as he worked on the *Rake's* conclusion (see example 5). And see example 6 for Tom's penitential Lenten statement in the madhouse duet with Ann: "In a foolish dream, in a gloomy labyrinth I hunted shadows disdaining thy true love; Forgive thy servant, who repents his madness. . . ."

And nobody could fail to hear a Passion chorale in Ann's final Duettino with her father, reinforced in its ritualistic solemnity by soft brass and implacable staccato strings in the bass: "Every wearied body must / Late or soon return to dust." To which her father rejoins: "God is merciful and just / God ordains what ought to be" (see example 7).

Is, then, the solemn spiritual tone at the end of this ostentatiously contrived opera achieved just by reference to sacred music and sacred text, despite the general message that there is no message, that all is play?

Surely it is in the very formality of the *Rake* that an objective force, a force of "God ordaining what ought to be," is promulgated. Throughout the libretto Auden and Kallman carefully build up symbolic mythological structures from several traditions, reinforcing the inevitability of the end, as if in Sophoclean tragedy. There seems to be no escape. The opera carries something of the timeless inevitability of myth (a timeless progress, paradoxically), which the very rigidity of a large number of closed musical structures hammers into place, as in a Byzantine mosaic.

Tom in the end chooses love, thus cheating the devil of his soul. The refinement of this great ending lies in the beautiful reconciliation of his free choice with its opposite, the inevitable decline and death of him who chose to be a rake, a defier of "Mother Nature," civilization's pathetic little hero. The opera is transparently civilized and artificial, its ties with show business are displayed for all to hear, thus disowning any personal authorial message. Yet because no one is telling us anything, what it means (and many of us probably register that it has deeper meaning than most twentieth-century operas) seems objective, immutable, above merely individual opinion. And this is to consider not just the "Bachian" ending, but the opera as a whole. One of Stravinsky's most famous remarks was "I am the vessel through which *Le Sacre* passed." One might with equal though opposite sense imagine him saying: "Other composers are the vessel through which *The Rake's Progress* passed." Again we may ask, just who is the composer?

At this point we must begin to make some finer distinctions. *The Rite of Spring*, to stay with Stravinsky a moment longer, has connotations of shamanism, of Dionysian ecstasy. The artist is, as it were, in a trance, *possessed* by a voice not his own; he's not his normal self. (Of course, Wagner too—to pick a typical romantic stance—intimated that his was a similar Dionysian possession, for instance in his letters to Mathilde Wesendonck about *Tristan* . . . though Richard Strauss, in typical manner, had a half-point when he said that the head that composed *Tristan* must have been as cold as ice.) The self-effacement of *The*

Rake's Progress, however, is a different sort of authorial absence. Here, it seems, Stravinsky is also saying "this is not me"; but he is implying something else as well, along the lines of "See my wit, I'm a good entertainer; my singers can perform and show off. This is a stratagem to delight; it will be fresh after the shabby emotions with which you were overladen before."

The tone of voice has changed. Whereas in the *Rite* we hear a shaman speaking, in the *Rake* we encounter an impresario. The one is unconscious, the other amusing. Neither is, presumably, the "central" self, though to an outsider both are genuine Stravinsky. The notion of "authorial absence" in fact implies some prior central self that has been (falsely) set up, taken to be the whole, and then perceived to have disappeared. These others, the shaman and the impresario, we excluded from the "whole" we took to be the center.

We—most composers, that is—generally have a good intuitive sense of what our central self is, our core. Nevertheless, from playful to profound, many levels take center stage from time to time, and we will accordingly assert or withdraw our core on the creative scene as seems fit. To others the withdrawal may not be apparent; they may still hear the characteristic voice.

Scrutiny will show how not only the area from which the core has withdrawn (that of the impresario and so on), but also the core itself, will have a high percentage of borrowed elements. The point of view of the composer, however, is that some of that material remains closer to us (our core) than other parts; that is, we establish a hierarchy of elements of self.

It should be added that running through composers' and artists' and writers' statements in history is the thread of the supremacy of the unconscious. The shamanistic mode of Stravinsky's *Rite,* Schoenberg's *Erwartung,* or any other extreme irruption of the so-called irrational is arguably more at the core than anything else. We didn't need Freud to tell us that, though he helped. Certainly the Romantics, to say nothing of earlier artists, saw reason as taking us away from our true selves.

"In order to understand anything," wrote Schubert, "we must

first believe in something; that is the highest basis on which feeble understanding first erects the pillars of proof. Intelligence is nothing else than analysed faith."[6] And Liszt wrote about what he called the "demon Thought": "Why all that desire to stunt and control natural and artistic impulses? The first time the little garden-artist mislays his shears, everything grows as it should and must."[7] A little later in history Ravel commented: "[It is a] relatively modern error . . . that leads people to think that the artistic instinct is directed by the will. . . . In art, craftsmanship in the absolute sense of the word cannot exist. In the harmonious proportions of the work, in the elegance of its unfolding, inspiration plays an almost unlimited role. The will to develop can only be sterile."[8] And Schoenberg, quoting Schopenhauer, wrote: "The composer reveals the inmost essence of the world and utters the most profound wisdom in a language which his reason does not understand."[9]

So, being "vessels" brings us back as "selves" into the picture, but at a deeper level, that of the unconscious, or intuition, or inspiration. The question must now be asked to what degree the unconscious is individual or collective. Is it "me," *my* unconscious, as Freud thought? Or is there some deeper connection, some seabed connecting the little individual islands we see poking up above the surface, some archetypal structure that is inherent in the mind, an innate grammar, a participatory epistemology resolving the self's despair at being cut off from knowing the world "in itself," as Jung and his followers posited? Whatever the answer, the place from which inspiration comes is undeniably unconscious. We cannot easily know much more than its borderlands.

Stockhausen, for one, places it unequivocally in the collective domain. As he says in this interview, he does not see the music he writes as his own in the usual sense:

> I just write the music as it comes intuitively into my mind, and I expect the musicians will begin to grasp that making music is a spiritual activity.
>
> *(Interviewer) Yes, but it's not only spiritual, is it? It's also intellectual.*

The rest is secondary because it is the technical aspect of the process. The main thing is that we create sounds so pure that they are a vessel for the cosmic forces—let's say the cosmic force that runs through everything.

But surely you are communicating, aren't you?

No, I'm not communicating anything personally. I'm just making music which makes it possible to make contact with this supra-natural world. As I said, the music is a vessel, a vehicle, which people can get tuned in to and discover their inner selves by, discover what they have forgotten about themselves.[10]

In this case, Stockhausen's level of creative mind may be described as lying where the intuitive core, the center, is assimilated to another center, a collective "cosmic force" that both is and is not Stockhausen. Artists and religions have spoken ceaselessly of the unitive state to which this artistic viewpoint is akin.

For the moment I will encourage you to be the sort of listener Stockhausen would like, participating in the collective by being utterly concentrated. He wants us not to be conscious *of* the music (dualistic) but to be conscious *as* the music (nondualistic). *We are the music.*

Summing up an interview in 1980, he said:

I hope that I have conveyed that we should concentrate to an exceptional extent on the process of listening itself—I have not wasted many words on describing what we hear. I attempted to make clear that we should concentrate to the greatest possible degree on the sound itself. I even said that we should become the sound. If the sound moves upwards I also move upward; if it moves downwards, I go down too. If it becomes quieter, so do I. If the sound divides itself into two, I follow suit, and meet myself again when the sound reunites, etc. This means that one is completely swallowed up in the process of listening. . . .

I would like to make clear something else: that we simply open up rather than create links between specific musical processes and certain feelings or states of being—sadness, joy, or wanting to dance. When that opening hap-

pens, one is modulated unceasingly by the music—
whether one wants that or not. Whether we are aware of
this or not, we are modulated by a specific piece of music
in a specific way. We become this music up to a certain
point, and we will never be the same again once we have
heard that music.[11]

Please listen, in a celebrated passage from *Kontakte* for
piano, percussion, and tape, to how you "are" a line—deconstructed into short impulses, reassembled in transformed guise
as meditational, spaced-out self—and how later your unified
layers are stripped off like an onion (in the tape part they
become streamers of staccato points) and eventually your selfhood is destroyed in deep crashes of sound. Destruction, says
Stockhausen, is always necessary for the creation of the new.

CD 14: Stockhausen, *Kontakte*

In this "overture" I've tried to clear some preliminary
ground, to make space for the concept of the "spiritual." The
"I" has been shown to be confusingly polyphonic—core vs.
non-core, playful vs. profound, singular vs. universal. Which is
it? Or is it all of them? But we must cover much ground before
we can tackle those questions head-on. In the next chapter I
will plunge into the heart of ambiguity and try to show that its
existence is crucial to our journey.

2

The Role of Ambiguity

Let us delve further into the mysterious nature of music—a notoriously difficult enterprise—in the hope of making the reason for its possible connection with the notion of spirituality clearer.

Consider example 8, the opening of a great symphony. Just an A, gently pulsating, but for the moment the center of the world. Next (see example 9) comes a harp figure involving F♯ below the A, the A itself, and B above it. The rhythm is more regular, and seems therefore to displace the irregular opening As: Ockham's Razor, the simplest way of construing the rhythmic data, prevails. The pitches, moreover, call the A itself into question: if by cultural conditioning or feelings of innate harmonic simplicity we thought that A was the tonic, the center, we now suddenly float away from that certainty. A new center, almost pentatonic in feel, has arisen.

That, in turn, is to be displaced by a more elaborate melodic structure in the horn (see example 10), which adds a D falling to a C♯, thus changing the pentatonic to the D major tonality, "suspended" on a dominant pedal—a different world again.

The horn melody is then displaced on center stage by a melody on the violins. All this "displacement" occurs only in the sense of moving from the center to the periphery, for these elements continue to exist. For the whole passage, see example 11.

Any music that is not monodic would have done to make the simple point that most material is characterized by ambiguity. Sometimes idea A is principal, sometimes secondary, and sometimes merely accompanimental: its role changes. Sometimes it even turns into idea B, then back again. This is hardly surprising given the small number of notes available (prior to microtuning systems). We see the thing-we-recognize change like a chameleon, sometimes seeming to hover between two things, equally close to both. At some deep level of perception and analysis, every idea is simultaneously every other idea. Axioms of conceptual reasoning aim to exclude such ambiguity; music, equally axiomatically—by its very nature—contradicts these precepts. The point is that just above that level, as musical ideas fluctuate between one state and an ambiguous other, we witness an ever-changing flux.

Life also may be characterized as an alternation of finding oneself in the center or at the periphery. According to Albert Low in his text *The Wounded Surgeon,* in a certain sense we are always at both. He writes: "I am at the center, but that to which I am central is also at the center and so I am peripheral to it, but I cannot be peripheral to it because I am at the center."[1] Low, a Zen master, ascribes most of the mental suffering in the world to this conflict. As all English children sing, "I'm the king of the castle, you're the dirty rascal." It's like a territorial battle, but between kings and spies. We are (center) and we look on (periphery). We participate, then abruptly we observe. When we look at the wiggly line called a Rubin profile, we see one face, then suddenly, after tension, we "flip" and see only the other face—but we know both are there. We have a mind, we have a brain: the mind interprets, forms, creates the world; the brain is the world, "matter," which is neurological and continuous with the rest of matter.

Science has plumbed to some extent the nature of the physical universe, yet all this discovery is achieved by and through human consciousness, which itself influences what is learned and about which we know next to nothing, including how it arises from the physical world. So do we know nothing about natural science? The question is inapposite, because the root of the problem lies in the ambiguity that is endemic in life, or rather (beyond that) in the sensing that there is a higher unity that contains ambiguity. It is my contention that music reveals this ambiguity and reconciles it in harmony, contains it.

We need not pause long over music's ability to unify contrasts, a feature, for instance, of sonata form in its classic guise, or of the interrupted cadence (V–VI), which combines maximum surprise with two out of three notes nevertheless the same as in the tonic chord (minimum surprise)—something characteristic of most European music since 1750.

It is interesting to note that the thinker who has come to be known as the revealer of Western tonal music's unity in complexity in the most fundamental way, Heinrich Schenker, had an important guide in scientific writings: specifically, those of Goethe—who wrote "to separate the unified, to unite the separated, is the life of nature. This is the eternal . . . inhaling and exhaling of the world in which we live, breathe and exist."[2] Goethe's famous vision of the prototypical *Urphänomen* was a spiritual, yet at the same time real—"with-my-own-eyes"—*aperçu:* a flash of insight that came after long contemplation of types of plant or animal or mineral. Schenker clearly echoes this process when writing of his vision of fundamental unity in music: "Religion, philosophy and science all press toward the shortest formula. A similar instinct led me to comprehend that the musical work too arises solely out of the core of the *Ursatz.* . . . I saw through to the *Urlinie,* I did not figure it out!"[3] Schenker's "seeing through" is a flash of intuitive observation, and the graphs and the much-maligned *Urlinie* are actually the result of what William Pastille calls "an elevated sense of hearing," which revealed the laws of tonal gravity to one deeply familiar with their workings, rather than being the perceptions of more normal hearing.

A quintessential theme in musical history even beyond the period of tonal music addressed by Schenker, and at least up to Boulez and Birtwistle, has been that the greater the contrasts successfully unified in a single work, the more important that work seems to be. In this sense, Beethoven's Ninth is more important than his First. Generally speaking, long great works are seen as greater than short great works, because they contain more to contrast and more to unite. This is in radical distinction to Indian music, for example, where an improvisation that goes on all night is not necessarily an indication of an exceptional achievement in the content.

Complex unity, then, is a paradigm of Western music. "The essential question that occupies the musician," Stravinsky said, "always and inevitably reverts back to the pursuit of the One out of the Many."[4] And Beethoven is reported by Bettina von Arnim as saying, "Music gives the mind a relation to the Harmony. Any single, separate idea has in it the feeling of the Harmony, which is Unity."[5]

If you hear this chord, for instance (see example 12), it means rather little. But let us place the chord in a work you probably know well as a whole—see example 13—and then hear it again by itself but mentally as *part* of a whole (see example 14).

Now the chord contains the entire *Eroica* Symphony by implication; it becomes charged with enormous meaning. Because of its place in a unified tonal system, a coherent thematic and harmonic trajectory, it cannot be pulled out and said to be just itself. Implicated in this detail is the entire work, just as an acorn contains an oak forest at a certain level of explicitness. Each level reveals in its time its full potential, it arrives on the surface, preceding and succeeding other levels by turns.

This smooth unfurling of the latent musical idea gives a different picture of human memory. My impression is that memory is made up of snapshots, discrete quanta, entities that are static. In this different picture, in what the physicist David Bohm calls "implicate order," we have a fluidity, a film sequence, a constant unfolding that connects images or, in our case, musical moments.[6] This is what Beethoven meant, and indeed many composers have expressed a similar awareness of latent unity.

But unity is not enough; or at least, it is too simplistically understood. Once, after I had given a lecture about Schenkerian principles of structural deep unity, the English composer Robin Holloway objected: "But it is the varying surface which is important, it is *that* which attracts and delights." Lutoslawski likewise used to emphasize that "the quality of the ideas is everything"—deep structural thinking is secondary. This distrust of depth might be the creed of many postmodernists today, in differing fields. Whatever one may think of postmodernism, it is high time that the prevailing orthodoxies of academic music are challenged. As Robert Adlington has noted, for too long music has been described in terms derived from verbal language and its modes of organization—narrative and plot, for instance—and in terms derived from visual concepts, like "form unfolding": structure seen in notation or imagined like an object or journey we move around or through. These are borrowed perspectives and they are inadequate for music, although an entire pedagogic culture is founded on them. The structure of music is not reducible to these other discourses. It is something much more profound, mysterious, and difficult to get at.

My teacher Hans Keller always used to emphasize that the conscious pursuit of unity was dangerously academic, more craft than art. He was after strong contrasts, pushing the tolerance of unity almost to the breaking point and trusting in the unconscious to achieve it. Keller had a background in Viennese psychoanalysis; he practiced free association daily for five years and came to consider it as a sort of model for the role of the unconscious in composition. The more suppressed the connection between musical quanta, the more interesting it was. Even so, he criticized some composers for lack of unity: at some level it was what he cared most deeply about. He also held that music appropriated the primary (primitive?) process and, in a manner that seemed respectably logical, in fact inverted the precepts of logic—a phenomenon only recently understood thanks to psychology. As Keller put it, "The Law of Contradiction says that A is not both B and not B: in music it must, axiomatically, be both. The Law of Excluded Middle says that A either is or is not B, whereas in music it goes without saying that A must have it both ways if it is to be meaningful."[7]

So music has to do with two things—with ambiguity. A drive to unity is there, but it must be by way of variety. Both must coexist, be held in vibrant tension—what Goethe called "dynamic unity." The unconscious is at least a metaphor for the darkness in which the process of creating such a vibrant tension takes place. I take no joy in composing if I set out in broad daylight knowing exactly what I want: I feel cheated of the adventure that makes music art. Instead each new work must grope out into some dark region, in which the imagination and the unconscious can operate together. It must be full of contradictions—of "uncertainties, Mysteries, doubts, without any irritable reaching after fact and reason," as the poet John Keats said.[8] It must live in ambiguity. Debussy put it quite plainly: "Music must come from the shadows."[9] And Mahler commented, "The creation and the genesis of a work is mystical from beginning to end since one—himself unconscious—must create something as though through outside inspiration. And afterwards one scarcely understands how it happened."[10]

The conflicts of ambiguity are only possible because of unity. As Arthur Koestler says in *The Act of Creation*, "two self-consistent but habitually incompatible frames of reference" come together as one, in a sense regressing to a more basic, more primitive plane of understanding. Koestler argues that there is a regression, clearly seen in biology when primitive forms such as the flatworm will regrow all their organs from one segment, which the gardener's spade has severed. This is only possible because the forms are primitive enough to be building blocks common to very different new structures. Low tells a story from the trenches of the First World War: "It was breakfast time, and in a British trench the soldiers were . . . brewing tea. A German patrol leaped into the trenches with fixed bayonets. A British soldier, terrified, automatically and without thinking held out a cup of tea to the German who was about to stab him. The German turned and fled."[11] When nations fight they must first agree on something to fight about. Conflict cannot exist without agreement, an agreement more fundamental than the conflict. To fight there must be cooperation.

I will come back to these themes of regression and darkness. But let's take the ideas of ambiguity and unity a little further. When I compose, I am pulling together these dark conflicts and contradictions in an intuitive drive toward the promised land of unity. When I listen, I follow these same processes in the music (whether my own or others'). A lot has been written about what music reflects, or does not reflect, in psychic life, in social life, and so on. Such accounts have mostly suffered from too static a portrayal of the listener. It's not a case of the solid listener witnessing a changing and fluctuating representation of some sort, nor does the music depict how the psyche works or express emotion in any simple sense. We are ourselves volatile; we are constantly changing. When we listen to music we, as well as the music, are on the move, constantly reconstituting our selfhood, redefining ourselves, perhaps more intensely than usual. To make this idea a little more concrete, see example 15, a passage that Mahler marks *Schattenhaft* (shadowy), then, a little later, *Allmählich an Ton gewinnend* (gradually winning back tone).

Mahler here leads the musical subject back from a shadowy existence to reconstitute itself in the D major Andante; we witness, we observe, this, but more important, we also participate in it as an experience. We are both objective and subjective, observing and creating, at the periphery and at the center—experiencing ambiguity. We observe the music's goals, its samenesses and ruptures, its attempts to create order in flowing time, its harmony. It is a model, a utopia. At the same time, we recognize that this integrated "subject" is never quite what we achieve in normal life, that the *struggle* in time is "truth." The time is social time, contingent: it is "subject-in-process" time.

But even as we observe these things, we participate in the existence of unity, in details as well as in the whole, beyond time.

As John Rahn puts it,

> Human life and music listened to by that life do not run parallel in straight lines never meeting, but rather intertwine closely, touching each other all over, each penetrating and being penetrated by the other, so that while they touch they almost fuse into one entity, one life-music or music-life. . . . The experience of music affords a person the chance to think without language, without snipping the experience into discrete "segments" wrapped up into "signifiers" and free of the consequent machinery of negation, polar oppositions such as subject/object, and the whole permutational heap of linguistic gravel whose constant grinding can be music to nobody's ears.[12]

The detail of Mahler's falling *Leb' wohl* Farewell 3–2 motive is a descent to what Julian Johnson calls the pentatonic embrace:[13] the 2, which hovers above its tonic without resolving, suggests an oceanic whole, gravity-defying, static, and timeless, as in the same motif at the end of *Das Lied von der Erde*, where it's a delicate reference to oriental holism combined with the word *ewig* (eternally) in the voice. The "isness" of the pentatonic—it doesn't need to go anywhere—obviously corresponded to Mahler's vision of an Orient beyond time, a space where restlessness could end.

The horrific death of the subject or self can be lived in a passage near the conclusion of the first movement of the Ninth Symphony. It is an extreme moment. It is followed by "sounds of chivalry—death in armor," as Berg described the fanfare of muted trumpets; they follow this cataclysm, with implacable formality. And then, slowly, the lyrically singing subject is reconstituted in harmony with the world. This primary pentatonic material, with its falling leading notes (C♯ *always* gently resolves to the pentatonic B), its falling 3–2, its reference to Beethoven's *Leb' wohl* as well as to the elegiac second subject of the slow movement of Beethoven's Ninth Symphony, its memory of *Parsifal*'s Grail Temple bells and their solemn promise of transcendence—this music is both a rebirth and a dissolution into wholeness, perhaps an emergence into something nearer nirvana than a new incarnation. The point is, both individuality (the subject-in-process) and dissolution are ambiguously present.

This "death of the subject" experience at the beginning of the next example is founded on a work Mahler had often conducted, *Götterdämmerung:* specifically, the moment when Siegfried is treacherously stabbed in the back, the dark peripeteia of the *Ring* cycle. Notice how close Hagen's falling semitone motive is to Mahler's subject—dangerously close, as if death is always just around the corner. The funeral march that follows in Mahler ("sounds of chivalry") refers harmonically to the curse motive that follows in the Wagner. Let me make that clear by following the Wagner *Götterdämmerung* passage (see example 16) with that from the Mahler symphony (see example 17).

Incidentally, the wild exhilaration of the Mahler just before it is cut low by the terrifying pulses of the trombones repeats, I have noticed, an early, little-known song at the words (Mahler's own) "O selige Stunden" (Oh blissful hours), an ecstatic and yet anguished outpouring of Mahler's unrequited love for Josephine Poisl thirty years earlier. Mahler was building his subjecthood from these, and probably many other, past fragments.

It is not necessary, of course, for us to know the sources of Mahler's memory, any more than it was necessary to deconstruct *The Riot* in the first chapter. As listeners, we respond from our own past memories, the shrapnel fragments embedded in our own buried psychic world that are summoned to life by sympathetic resonance with the vibrations of the music. They awaken and form a dance together, gathering around a nucleus of connecting imaginative energy. One person will remember a childhood adventure, another will relive a romantic moment, another will recall a crisis or trauma—though the memories may consist of little more than the traces of these experiences, their surface detail being no longer recoverable. For musicians, these traces will be strongly associated with other music. And of course, musicians will be aware of the formal unity; they will be "expert listeners," to use Adorno's term, who grasp long spans of energy evolution and perceive all that's there in terms of repetition, transformed repetition, and background structure such as tonality and harmonic fields. These expert-listener matters, too, are constituting the self, which is ever moving, always searching for the experience of wholeness. As one moves through a piece one knows well, one tastes the delicious flavor of unity (if the piece encourages it); one is moving and moved, yet also still, part of a promised harmony. At the end, the profound satisfaction of a mysterious insight possesses one. It seems as if the answer has been found. Unity *contains* ambiguity. Because the insight is not final, however, listeners listen to more music, and composers go on to compose again, and try to do better in new compositions. To quote Low: "Music does not express emotions. Emotion is the response to ambiguity, the multiplicity of Unity."[14] Music certainly may sound "sad," "joyful," but that is not the same as "expressing" emotions. Hegel said, "The special task of music is that, in presenting any content to the mind, it presents it neither as it is latent in consciousness as a general concept, nor as a definite external form offers itself elsewhere to observation or is through art more completely represented, but rather in the way in which it becomes alive in the sphere of subjective inwardness."[15] In other words, music is neither an abstraction nor an outer object but an inner coming-to-life of something (beyond subject/object differences).

We sense the dynamic of sharpened and flattened fourth, of major or minor third, of leading note: a dynamic, in fact, that seems neither exclusively outside nor inside ourselves. Pitches seem to embody a flavor, a color, one might even say a spiritual nature, when they are defined by another pitch or other pitches as parts of intervals. A major sixth has a certain feel, a supertonic has a certain feel, and moving through pitches and intervals in tonal, as well as atonal or microtonal, music (though most clearly in a field of tonality, no matter how fleeting), one experiences a dynamic energy that is neither exclusively inner nor outer, neither subjective nor objective, but straddles an ambiguity.

Is the dynamic in the sound (see example 18) or in us? Remember the fanciful story of Mozart's being unable to sleep because someone had played an unresolved dominant seventh: he rushed desperately downstairs and found his peace—see example 19. Is this effect of the dominant seventh a cultural artifact or a phenomenon of Nature, valid universally?

The science of acoustics will show that the dominant seventh is less fundamental than the perfect triad, the lowest of the harmonics in the harmonic series. The perfect triad is "home." But acoustics will also show that (given a little approximation in the seventh harmonic) the dominant seventh is fairly fundamental too; in other words, it can sound resolved, as in much spectral music of today—Grisey's, Murail's, Lindberg's, and some of my own, for example. So evidently Mozart lived lower down the harmonic series than we do; also, he didn't use the microtones many of us love in our music nowadays, which come still higher up the series.

Is it therefore a matter of different cultures giving different dynamics to this dominant seventh? I don't think so, not entirely. I, who work in spectra a good deal, still hear its pristine dynamic with Mozart's sense of disturbance, especially in a Mozartean context. It is as if we can shift the spotlight to focus up and down the series to find our cultural home, but we cannot forget what is there even though it is not spotlighted. The eighteenth-century dominant seventh is explicable, materially, scientifically, but we also experience it inwardly, as a disturbance or a dynamic drive. It is matter and it is mind.

And if that ambiguity is too technical to be easily comprehensible, think of the Buddhist koan "Does the ear go to the sound, or the sound to the ear?" In other words, where does the mind stop and the object start? Zen Buddhists maintain that koans are to be used to crack open normal, logical modes of thinking; because no logical answer is possible, something greater appears: an enlightened understanding—the unity in ambiguity. (Try this: touch the paper in front of you and try to say where the sensation in the finger ends and the paper begins. You may be nonplussed!)

The matter/mind relationship is actually a commonplace subject in music. Scores are written and performers perform oscillating between the two poles, blurring the distinction. Consider, for example, the difference between intervallic performance and physical performance. In intervallic performance, the string quartet, vocal consort, or other group capable of refined tuning performs with little or no vibrato, enjoying the pure Pythagorean, mathematical proportions of good intonation. In physical performance, by contrast, the performers concentrate on their instruments—on rich tone, using vibrato that may span intervallically outrageous amounts and tuning that is emotively twisted, with gestures of arm, body, or voice expressively to the fore. The "grain" of the singer's voice, to use Barthes's expression, gives the message, which is personal rather than universal—Jessye Norman, not Pythagorean. The body of the source is clearly "in" the sound. According to Curt Sachs, in primitive cultures narrow-range, speechlike, emotional melodies are often found side by side with wider-interval, quasi-pentatonic, formal melodies.[16] Most sophisticated Western music, too, plays on the ambiguous border between these two qualities. A good quartet, playing tonal music, will clearly "breathe" in and out both mathematical beauty and physical-emotional gesture, according to the forms and passions of the score. The more distant triads and altered chords in the middle of a phrase, for example, may thus be much more "mistuned" than those at the beginning and at the cadence.

The mental/physical ambiguity in music has also become emphatic in another, and rather important, dimension: timbre or color. This dimension begins to fill in the gap created by the weakened force of tonality's dynamism in composition since Schoenberg and the Darmstadt School.

If we look at music from a couple of points of view, this will become clear. The activity of listening to form is largely a mental one: we add one note to another, one phrase to another, until eventually they stand in the memory as a structure. We choose which notes to connect with which others to satisfy our desire for rich meaning. We could try to listen to Haydn serially or, if we are Chinese, according to traditional Chinese musical syntax; whatever way it is, we make a choice and store the outcome in mental space.

There is also a less mental way to listen, and that is to be concerned not with memory and form, but with the "now," with the color and flavor of the moment. Although, as we've seen, all music has a dynamic, a sense of tension, it *is* occasionally possible to nudge music out of its context and hear it vertically, rather than as a horizontal line. Obviously, the music must invite this mode of perception. Obviously, too, elements of it must be virtually static, or at least very slow; otherwise the discourse, the argument of melody and polyphony, will be too domineering. One must be able to get inside the sound itself, not hear it as a passing element belonging to structure.

Please listen, by way of illustration, to the slow, slow end of my *Madonna of Winter and Spring* for orchestra with live electronics (1986). After thirty minutes that often involve much activity, much argument and discourse, we come to a stasis. The waves of sound are slowly moving around the hall (the blessing of the Madonna).

CD 15: *Madonna of Winter and Spring*

Madonna of Winter and Spring has the form of a meditation, or spiritual evolution: the four sections are titled "Conflict," "Descent," "Depths," and "Mary." "Depths" is like a dark night of the soul, almost empty of content, and "Mary" is a spring-like illumination, finishing, as you heard, with something oceanic, mystical. A type—one type—of spiritual trajectory or evolution is the inspiration for the form. The inspiration for the spirit of the work as a whole comes from a powerful experience. I was wondering what to do for my Henry Wood Promenade Concert commission for a work for orchestra and electronics. The *Mabinogion*, scenes from the life of Christ, music from the "other side," the world of Amphortas contrasted with a spiritualized view of suffering—many such subjects flew chaotically through my mind and were duly noted in my sketchbook, though whether any but myself would be made aware that they played a part in the music remained to be decided. A portrait of Mary, of what she means in the world as I saw it, was only one of several possibilities—but a touching one. One day after Eucharist at my local church in Lewes my eye alighted on a statue of Mary above the altar and I found myself asking quite simply if she would wish me to write music in her honor. To my delighted surprise the statue distinctly moved and with a most beautiful gesture indicated clearly that she would. I had an extraordinary sense of contact with another, love-filled, world. It happened—significantly, I felt— on Mothering Sunday, March 17, 1985. I still feel the breath of that encounter twelve years later.

What is the relation of art to spiritual evolution? Of course, it is often a prerequisite of great art that it uplifts in some way. In the presence of what we respond to as "great art" we experience a loss of self, a loss of the observer. And that sort of transcendence of the narrow ego may be called, even in the case of "depressing" or tragic art, the uplift of spirit, or *participation mystique.*

Experiencing the subtle dialectic of discourse and spirit, where one leads into and is unified with the other, is the gift of intelligent and sensitive listening. In *Madonna of Winter and Spring*, this dialectic is explicitly the subject of the work itself. *Madonna* moves clearly from discourse to spirit.

It may be objected that "spirit"—however we define it—can only be latent within a manifestation, rather than portrayable as such. Thomas Mann (that hypersophisticate!) once said that all artists must be just a little naive. I have no compunction in singing of what is most charming, no hesitation in trying to portray, sometimes as directly or naively as possible, the experience of spirit itself— always failing, of course, because in the end it is true: spirit has to be mediated.

But the attempt is crucial. It is my obsessive song.

Broadly speaking, spirit *underlies* discourse. It is the Ground, the All, the background level of the Schenkerian tree, which contains everything, all discourse, yet which seems almost empty of content. It is the Silence out of which every sound is born. As Rilke exhorts in the "First Duino Elegy": "Listen to the news that ceaselessly arises out of silence."

In *Madonna of Winter and Spring* this "silence" is represented by stasis, by prolongation. The reverberator grabs sounds here and there from the orchestra and prolongs them, often while the orchestra is continuing with its discourse. The background harmonic field surfaces for a while, and then submerges, suggesting that it is there all the time, underneath.

At the end the conductor is requested to "lose all sense of time" in holding a succession of fermatas. A harmonic field, extracted from the brass fanfares by the reverberator, alternates in very slow waves with the synthesizers, which articulate the same harmonic field with constant filter changes. The mind settles to such a degree that it lives in the sound, freely experiencing the spectra. The spatial diffusion is also slow and calming, the two waves' sounds moving through each other in different directions throughout the hall.

So the notion that spirit underlies discourse is clarified, spelled out, by the exposure of spirit when discourse dies down. If the thematic or formal argument never faded to the background (as in most music from Bach to Schoenberg), the immanence of spirit in music might be less consciously perceived, or perceived only in the other sphere we have discussed, that of formal unity, the Harmony.

The idea that "music is the play of the Relative on the Ground of the Absolute" is therefore what gives me joy in composing. That is the not-so-hidden "message" of *Madonna of Winter and Spring.* Music is not *basically* unchanging Ground, nor is it only surface conflict and play; it is a third thing, a special quality of liberated tension.

Another "message" of the work concerns of course the importance of the feminine. Humankind is a tiny speck in a vast complex of galaxy clusters, and even on Earth we are only a minuscule proportion of the planet's evolution, a product, seemingly, of genetic randomness. We are unable to access truth because of our concept-making mind, through which the world impinges, and our observation of objects changes the objects as we observe them. The crisis of alienation and isolation that such a worldview has precipitated is essentially a masculine crisis, created by men in a patriarchal system using characteristically male modes of analysis. The world we see, that we acknowledge, is the world we create: and it is largely a male one. To understand that we are *part* of a world that is *creating itself*, however, is a feminine understanding: an understanding based in wholeness, community, intuition, connection, healing, emotion, ambiguity. The reunion of masculine and feminine is the still obscure revolution of paradigms that we secretly long for. The radical importance of feminism, which may provide important philosophical tools for effecting this revolution, has scarcely begun to be recognized.

Madonna, like many of my works, is also concerned with breathing, because breathing is not only the vehicle of life but also the day-to-day physical and sonic representation of states of emotion. In music's onomatopoeic imitation of its speeds and shapes, we have one of the clearest symbols of human psycho-physical experience. In *Madonna* (as in other works) I also wanted to make a further, deeper, metaphoric use of breathing, that to which St. John of the Cross refers in the lines "And in thy sweet breathing, full of blessing and glory, / How delicately thou inspirest my love!"[17]

The "breathing of God," to which St. John alludes, is something that is experienced by many mystics, oriental and Western alike. In it the "normal," individuated world, in slow, rhythmic oscillation, dissolves into "sheets of transparent flame" and back again to solid material.[18] It's as if the particle structure, or the pure energy, of matter becomes perceptible. I wanted to compose slow breathing rhythms, in which the inhalation comprised distinct form and the exhalation was luminescent, formless. Form and luminescence thus alternated in gently varying duration-spans of breath.

Let us finally return to the idea of color, or as it is represented in the new thinking, spectralism, in music: the art of composing with harmonic and inharmonic series, fused conglomerates of sounds.

One would not want to echo Boulez's "Inutile!" when he described those not acquainted with serialism; nevertheless, I find those contemporary composers who are completely untouched by spectralism less interesting than those who are. History seems grand, for once; spectralism has effected a fundamental shift: music will never be quite the same again. Spectral music is symbiotically allied to electronic music; together they have achieved a rebirth of perception. Yet while electronic music is a well-documented technological breakthrough, spectralism in its simplest form, as color-thinking, is a spiritual breakthrough.

Linguistic theory has made it abundantly clear that language is a somewhat limiting symbolic system. Those, like Julia Kristeva, who have brought psychoanalysis into this picture supplement the "symbolic" world with the "semiotic" world, a world prior to the dictates of the constitution of the speaking subject. Kristeva relates the semiotic to Plato's *chora*, or receptacle: a formless, incomprehensible entity that receives everything and in some mysterious way partakes of the intelligible. The survival of the "infant" within us can be seen in, among other things, the poetry of Mallarmé. Kristeva describes the effect of his work thus: "Indifferent to language, enigmatic and feminine, this [semiotic] space underlying the written is rhythmic, unfettered, irreducible to its intelligible verbal translation; it is musical, anterior to judgment, but restrained by a single guarantee: syntax."[19]

The equivalent for Mallarmé's enigmatic "music" in music itself is largely timbre, a nondiscursive element. Wagner, too, spoke of "the sea of harmony," the "Mother element," an "inmost dream . . . belonging to neither Space nor Time [which] remains the inalienable element of music, [whereas] through the rhythmic sequence of his tones in time the musician reaches forth a plastic hand, so to speak, to strike a compact with the waking world of appearances."[20] The symbolic mediator of the semiotic (primary) world, that which renders it intelligible, is "rhythm" in Wagner and "syntax" in Mallarmé.

Wagner, the master of harmony, himself developed into a protospectralist—for instance in *Parsifal,* where the real vision, it always seems, is one of timbre: the transcendence offered by the Holy Grail is not couched in terms of developed harmony (that is reserved for suffering, by and large) but in terms of timbre, of orchestration based on common chords magically transmuted to harmonic series, to spectra.

Here, in *Parsifal,* for the first time, there is no distinction between harmony and timbre. Harmony is timbre; timbre is harmony.

Spectralism, like harmony, is in essence outside the world of linear time. In music, time is articulated by rhythm; in psychology, time is articulated by the process of chopping up and arranging experience into language, which separates us from the primary world and joins us to the linear symbolic order.

But the fascination of spectral thinking is that it, too, can easily shift into the realm of linear time, into melodic thinking: there is a large borderland of ambiguity to exploit. It is not a question of forsaking harmony and regarding everything as timbre, as some French composers do, but rather of harmony being subsumed into timbre. Intervallicism can shade into and out of spectralism, and it is in this ambiguity that much of the richness in the approach lies. In several of my own works, to offer a simple example, violins provide upper harmonics to a louder, lower fundamental, but at a given moment they cease to fuse, begin to vibrate, begin to move with independent intervals, and then ultimately return to their previous state. They are by turns faceless team members and distinguished individuals. The images of union and individuation are powerful ones, with both psychological and mystical implications (Stravinsky's "the many and the One").

Here is an excerpt from my work *Song Offerings* (1985), a set of divine love songs. The text, by Rabindranath Tagore, at this point is: "And for this thy love loses itself in the love of thy lover, and there art thou seen in the perfect union of two"—a union of two (or more) polyphonic voices in a fused spectrum: a union of two beings.

CD 16: *Song Offerings,* third movement

Tagore's bride/bridegroom imagery unfolds in a sequence, "expectation—dance of celebration—union—union in death," which is represented musically by an anacrusis (first song) sliding slowly up to C above middle C. The two central songs then explore that pitch as an axis, and the final song expands symmetrically outward from that axial pitch to the outer edges of musical space at the end. The C in this final song is sung to the word *death* several times near the beginning, and there is a particular acoustic reason for this. The vowel of the word *death* has an acoustic formant that makes prominent the third partial, a high g6, which is reinforced above the singer by the violin. Significantly, we have heard nothing but this same g6 from the beginning of the movement, eight bars before. Moreover, that note follows systematically from the previous movement, where the pitches climb up the symmetrical harmonic field, which has been clearly established, arousing strong expectations of the next highest note—the g6—to occur, after a brief pause between movements. It is also the only pitch played by the crotale, an instrument that enters at the end of the third movement. In other words, this pitch, systematically approached, timbrally prioritized, turns out to be *acoustically* linked to the structure of the phoneme *death*—it is revealed (when the voice later sings) to be the "death-note." So syntax, spectral acoustics, and poetry are inextricably linked.

It is this aesthetic of spectral hide-and-seek that has preoccupied me in my writing in the last few years. For instance, in

One Evening for two singers, instruments, electronics, and tape (Westdeutscher Rundfunk, 1993), the first movement is constructed intervallically—on the principle of symmetrical inversion around an axis. This principle gives a poised, floating stillness to the harmony, which changes but yet remains still around a central point, clearly sung by the singers:

CD 17: *One Evening,* first movement

The music is then repeated with the addition of very deep, soft notes on a synthesizer. In these pitches I found the most plausible fundamentals for a reading of the (symmetrical) harmony as *partials,* that is, spectrally. So the floating harmonies acquire a ghostly hierarchization, they become rooted, earthed: it is intervallicism seen in spectral light, the symbolic world seen in the larger perspective of the semiotic one, "enigmatic and feminine." Or as it says in the text, by the Tang dynasty poet Han Shan:

> Clear and empty shines the ocean like moonlight on snow,
> no trace of man nor gods.
> When the diamond eye is opened the mirage disappears
> and into stillness vanishes the earth.
>
> You will see that your body and mind,
> like the mountains, rivers, spaces, and territories
> of the outer world, are all contained inside
> the true mind, wonderful and illumined.

CD 18: *One Evening,* first movement

In a recent piano and tape work, *Tombeau de Messiaen* (1994)—homage to a protospectralist!—the taped portion consists of twelve pianos all tuned in harmonic series, each based on one of the twelve pitch-classes. The solo piano itself remains normally tuned, but when the balance is good (so that taped and live pianos are indistinguishable) the live piano has the role of providing the grit, the resistance to the spectra without seeming to be altogether outside them, partly because it quite often plays the same, or in other places nearly the same, spectral pitches.

CD 19: *Tombeau de Messiaen*

The fact of partly not fitting makes the discourse interesting for me, for it changes constantly from spectral fusion to microtonal polyphony and back. Either of these principles without the other seems a less rich, less attractive option for composition as I see it now.[21]

In my most recent works I have, however, begun to explore a deeper level of spectralism. In *Advaya* for cello and electronics (1994), research that I did at IRCAM led to a new structural order. IRCAM had recently developed the capacity to analyze sound, say a vibrant note or melody, and convincingly resynthesize it in a form in which the plethora of data was manageable and manipulable. The digital resynthesis tracked the partials of the notes, faithfully following all vibrato, jitter, and changes of color. Addressing such questions as where to transpose each tracked partial by, for instance, adding a certain amount of frequency to each and achieving new inharmonicity, I realized that if the amount added to each of the, say, forty partials in use was the *same*, then periodically the original harmonic series would reduplicate itself as the amount progressively increased. But it reduplicated itself each time with one more lowest partial missing. At these goalpost points each original partial had been multiplied by 2, 3, 4, 5, etc., and so had shifted up the series one notch. A sense of sameness, yet of lightening, occurs in this spectral world, very comparable to the sense of rising by octaves in the world of single notes.

What if one sticks to this seemingly basic acoustic operation of equal-amount addition and explores the interstices between the "octaves"? In between lie the *in*harmonic spectra, which, it turns out, are compressed into smaller steps than those of the harmonic series. If, say, 50hz is added to a fundamental—say of 100hz—the pitch rises a large musical interval, a perfect fifth, to 150hz; adding 50hz to the tenth partial, 1000hz, however, raises the pitch only a very small interval, to 1050hz, about a quarter-tone So the bass shoots up while the treble scarcely moves, thus "compressing" the natural intervals. Until, that is, they correspond to the next set of natural intervals; at that point the interval between the tenth and eleventh partials can be heard to have become exactly the interval between the natural eleventh and twelfth partials.

Exploring these new compressions I was fascinated to find that the amount added affected the sonic result in a beautifully simple, Pythagorean way. Taking a cello note of 220hz (open A string), if I added half that value, 110hz, the fundamental moved up a perfect fifth to 330hz and the inharmonic partials produced a harmonious, near harmonic spectrum, close in sound to the natural series. If a third of 220hz were added, a slightly less harmonious spectrum resulted; if a quarter, again slightly less. If I added something very complex like 11/17 of 220hz, then a rough spectrum, dissonant and complex, sounded. In other words, exactly the same subjective results were obtained as occurs with single-note intervals: 3:2 generates a pleasing "pure" fifth, 4:3 a "pure" fourth, and 17:11 an out-of-tune dissonant minor sixth or overlarge perfect fifth. So the spectral domain obeys exactly the same laws as the intervallic domain. Rough or smooth sounds result from the same ratios.

I also found—and this is important for composition—that just as in tonality the smooth chords (the "common chords") head the hierarchy in which the rough chords (the "altered" chords) fill many subordinate levels, approximately speaking, so a clear hierarchy emerged in the *spectral* space. Natural series pin the range of spectra into place as marking out a well-ordered, easily audible sonic world: this world describes a range never heard until computer techniques of resynthesis became, in the nineties, precise enough to make it possible.

I found myself thinking again in terms of tonic (no addition to the partials), dominant (the case where 3/2 of the fundamental is added to each partial), subdominant (the 4:3 case), and mediant (5:4). A twist of the spiral indeed. . . . The mathematically related interval system that has dominated world music from at least Pythagoras on has been reborn in completely new terms. Any child can hear it.

All that has been said can similarly be applied to subtraction of equal amounts, which generates equivalent *expanded-interval* spectra.

It can also be applied in the time sphere. Stockhausen, in his famous article "How Time Passes" and works such as *Gruppen* and *Inori*, applied the principles of serialism to time, relating speeds of frequency (pitches) to speeds of tempo. Pitches and tempi were related *to one another*, for the first time ever, in an all-pitches-are-equal serial field. My system is closer to tonal thinking (and the harmonic series), with all tempi related to a *fundamental* tempo. Tempi that differ from any "basic" one in use for a particular section are always heard *against* it: for instance, 7 in the time of 6 basic beats would be the time equivalent of a compression of the natural series made by adding 1/6 of the fundamental frequency to each partial. So the relation to the fundamental speed is audibly measurable (with clear degrees of "complexity"), just as the relation to the natural spectrum is always audibly measurable in terms of degree of dissonance.

Each inharmonic spectrum can be analyzed by the computer for its virtual fundamental: the computer asks what is the highest possible bass frequency that could be a fundamental to all partials of that spectrum understood as an incomplete *natural* harmonic series. Sometimes it supplies a very low fundamental frequency, indicating that the spectrum consists of very high partial numbers, perhaps in the hundreds or even thousands. Sometimes it supplies a higher fundamental frequency, in which case the spectrum is a group of partials fairly far down the harmonic series and accordingly will sound less rough; in that case the partials may lie in the twenties, thirties, forties, and fifties, for instance. Clearly there is, strictly speaking, no such thing in this system as a truly inharmonic spectrum; it is just that some are clustered higher (much higher) up the ladder of partials than others, so of course they sound inharmonic.

The history of music has been viewed by some as the slow ascent of humans up the harmonic series—with Xenakis and Scelsi we reached the thirty-second, for instance (to parody slightly). In my system that climb itself is the substance-matter of the syntax.

In *Ashes Dance Back* for choir and electronics (1997), I tried to reflect Rumi's poetry of ecstatic self-dissolution in Nature by using a simple sequence of equal-addition compression spectra, ranging from the natural series to its double one notch higher, the natural series' fundamental having been left behind. This was done by means of symmetrical additions of 1/8 of the fundamental frequency, then 2/8, then 3/8, 4/8, and so on up to 8/8. These rising formations—with the smooth 4/8 in the middle—were resyntheses of a vocal note with all its human irregularities preserved intact. Through that mass of data—translated into narrow band-pass filter openings—I blew recordings of real wind, fire, and water, so choral sound comes to be intermodulated with these elements. The element-permeated choir is therefore heard to dissolve into the processes of Nature: to be turbulently blown by wild wind, consumed by fierce fire, and finally lapped and healed by soothing, sparkling water. It lives in the unified nature of sound, both acoustically and spectrally, with no divisions.

Here are the expansions, moving from additions of 0/8 through 1/8, 2/8, and so forth to 8/8, followed by one of these expansions animated by recorded wind:

CD 20: "Sketches" for *Ashes Dance Back*

And here is an excerpt from *Ashes Dance Back* itself, where the 8/8 is attained and celebrated, together with the 5/8 and 6/8:

CD 21: *Ashes Dance Back*

Center/periphery, inner/outer, mental/physical, discourse/timbre: we have begun to scratch the dualist surface of how life and music are related and why music is so mysterious and real to us. Next we'll examine more closely the nature of dynamic unity.

3

Unity

George Steiner, in his book *Real Presences,* states his belief that
"ours is the long day's journey of the Saturday," referring to the
day between the crucifixion and the resurrection.[1] Some years
before I came across that passage I was asked to compose
images and music for any day in Holy Week I chose for a TV
film series. I somehow felt compelled to choose Saturday too.
Much of the resulting film was given over to static chanting
and an image of the body of Jesus lying in a rough sepulcher,
with nothing happening. It is a time of waiting, of emptiness,
with hints of redemption invisibly present. Yet as Steiner
points out, it is a disturbingly tense and topical time as well.

Steiner's book shows how language has reached an apparent "degree zero." Mallarmé evokes this emptiness in the
phrase "l'absence de toute rose"—the absence of any rose from
the word *rose*: that is, the separation of the signifying word
from the signified object. The resulting feeling is one of meaning in crisis. The modernists, Steiner asserts, were moving
toward the end of literature. According to them, language is a
prison compound built around us at an early age in which all
we can do is honestly acknowledge it and play a few games.
Although he accepts the truth of this position, Steiner finds it
ensnared by its own problem (namely, the connection of lan-

guage with meaning), and he hears a cosmic echo like that which astronomers detect, a residue of archetypes that, with goodwill, can be apprehended. He confesses there is no proof, that this residue exists, yet argues that there is no other explanation for great art, and in particular music. It is an impassioned plea, on which much depends.

It seems to me as well that to understand music fully (and perhaps to begin to understand the spiritual at all), we have to understand what language has done to us, following all the arguments through modernism, deconstruction, poststructuralism, and psycholinguistics to where we stand today. The best guide in this will have to be an artist, and preferably a practitioner of meditation. I can only point the way. Musical meaning, Steiner writes, "carries with it what . . . spiritual cognizance we can have of the core-mystery . . . that we are."[2]

I mention meditation because it gives insight into the crucial notion of pure awareness, in which one is aware, but aware of nothing. Eastern philosophy differs from Western in its reliance on experience of states of consciousness: one experiences the philosophy rather than thinks it (though some have argued that this puts it outside the scope of philosophy proper). Pure awareness is prior to subject/object duality, or ultimately, in enlightened meditation, posterior to it. When awareness of the world around arises, the tension in the I/other ambiguity increases to the point where stability is sought through language, and the "word," which seems to fix and order things, becomes paramount. In due course it divides the world up according to certain perspectives and leads on to reason, logic, and practical and scientific knowledge.

Music, however, exposes this ambiguity within language-based consciousness. It undoes the "word" and returns to pure awareness—or at least it gives a glimpse of it.

Remember how John Rahn put it: "The experience of music affords a person the chance to think without language, without snipping the experience into discrete 'segments' wrapped up into 'signifiers' and free of the consequent machinery of negation, polar oppositions such as subject/object."[3]

As Albert Low says, music is about "one knowing."[4] In that phrase, *one* is both subject and object: "knowing one thing" and "one person knowing" are rolled into a single notion. "One who knows" would be to bring back duality, but in the phrase "one knowing" we can sense the unity we experience in music when we lose ourselves in the awesome, higher harmony that music can be. Busoni once spoke of the way "great artists" played their own works differently at each performance, remodeling them on the spur of the moment "always according to the given conditions of that 'eternal harmony.'"[5] Liszt felt that music has "an existence not determined by man's intention. . . . It exists and flowers in various ways in conformity with basic conditions whose inner origin remains just as much hidden as does the force which holds the world in its course."[6]

This mysterious harmony or unity behind the varied details seems to be something prior to them, indeed prior to language. Psycholinguistics, particularly in its movement from Lacan to Kristeva in Paris, finds deep significance in the psyches of preverbal children. They are, in this theoretical perspective (which sometimes seems amazingly close to the Lankavatara Sutra and other ancient Buddhist texts), a key to understanding the constitution of the subject, the exile from the garden of Eden. Our consciousness before and after we acquire language parallels human awareness before and after the Fall. Preverbal existence is empty, but full of richness.

W. B. Yeats wrote of two wells. The dry well, which has a desiccated tree standing nearby, fills only rarely and then with difficulty; it stands for complete mystical unity, the renunciation of the lower for the higher self, the difficult way. The other well, the full well with a green tree at its edge, represents unity of being; harmony within the two lower planes of existence, those of integrated personality and sensuality; a happier way. Yeats described how Cuchulain missed seeing the dry well fill up because he was asleep, though he had traveled far in search of that water; in this manner Yeats symbolized his own spiritual failure to choose the difficult higher way. Indeed, Yeats compared himself with William Morris, who wrote of an earthly paradise, rather than Shelley, Rosetti, and the early Christians, or Malory and Wagner, who sought the austere Holy Grail of the unearthly paradise.[7]

Kristeva and her colleagues don't make the same distinctions, but the relationship between regression to the womblike well, to preverbal "maternal" existence, and regression to a different sort of emptiness, one that is a springboard to higher, egoless maturity and of which the saints and mystics speak, is clearly a crucial tone in musical expression. It is quite explicit in Wagner.

In *Parsifal* we experience both tendencies—a fact that, in my eyes, qualifies that opera as a sacred work of art. Parsifal, the pure innocent, easily resists the Flowermaidens in act 2, but on encountering Kundry he very nearly surrenders to an earthly paradise. The level of libido to which the Flowermaidens attempt to lure Parsifal is relatively lightweight; what Kundry suggests is much stronger. She invokes his childhood relationship to his mother. She does this, paradoxically, by means of language, calling him Parsifal, a name he once in childhood heard his now long-since dead mother call him. It is the first time this word has appeared in the opera. It is like a call from the dead, from beyond, awakening long-forgotten knowledge. More powerfully, however, Kundry does it by means of music, which interrupts the commotion of the Flowermaidens by halting rhythmic and melodic discourse. The music becomes suddenly still; we experience pure harmony. A subtle shift from major to minor modality moves us to the inner life, from the jolly badinage with the Flowermaidens to the deep recesses of childhood memory and the oceanic maternal unity of life at that time. Kundry then continues, lilting Parsifal back in time and consciousness, with a 6/8 lullaby (see example 20).

Of course, Parsifal finally resists Kundry's seduction and chooses the dry well; the earthly paradise of the womb is rejected for the harder way of selfless maturity—and ultimately the path of spiritual wisdom, the Unitive Way.

There are many instances in Wagner's oeuvre of paths of regression to earthly or heavenly paradise (and I take paradise to be virtually synonymous with unity): consider Venus and Elizabeth in their relation to Tannhäuser; Erda, the mysterious earth-goddess of *Das Rheingold*, who unexpectedly unnerves Wotan, thus hinting at the flexibility of the unconscious, of which his rigid principles are so oblivious; and, most interesting of all, Isolde, who is the cause of Tristan reliving his childhood in his great monologues of act 3. His new understanding of childhood illuminates the meaning of the love potion, that which causes the lovers to sink into union and ultimately the oblivion of the "World's Night." Here, too, ambiguity is "contained": the ambiguity of "day," the outer objective world with its social normality, and of "night," the inner, subjective world with its spiritual realm. Both are transcended in the *Liebestod*, the "one knowing" beyond: "In dem wogenden Schwall, in dem tönenden Schall, in des Welt Atems wehendem All."

Music, then, may emphasize unity in stasis, in lack of discourse, or in background coherent structure. Music that emphasizes ambiguity may well be more playful and witty, promulgating ingenuity and foreground structures; or it may seek to inspire violent emotional arousal.

Such ambiguity can be painful. Freud believed that only a tranquil, unaroused human was healthy, and that art was a therapy to extirpate threatening conflicts. Schopenhauer, too, believed that the only goal worth pursuing was release from the will, from the striving libidinal force within. Wagner misunderstood the Buddhist concept of nirvana and allied it with pessimism, a dark state of rest; nevertheless, it was a powerful ideal in his mind as well.

Nietzsche, on the other hand, espoused the aesthetic vision, with all the arousal, striving, and excitement it can contain, as the only true goal in life. Jung proposed integration and fullness, the "pleroma," likewise commending arousal or something like it as an aim.

Adherents on either side can be endlessly listed; but the mistake most make is to suppose that arousal is opposed to tranquillity. Of course music excites emotion, arouses incipient muscular movements. But music is profound as an art form precisely because it can do those things even within a tranquil framework. It is both emotionally intense and possessed of a deep sense of harmony, in the broad meaning of the word. The greater the conflicts it successfully unifies, the more spiritual the music.

This, perhaps, is why music is healing. Much tantalizingly equivocal evidence has been reported from EEG (electroencephalograph) monitoring of listeners, of how the brain hemispheres synchronize, of how the more peaceful brain waves flood the brain, and so on.

In his book *Awakenings,* Oliver Sacks movingly recounts— in a sense echoing the Bedlam scene in *The Rake's Progress,* where the inmates are soothed by Ann's heavenly singing— how his pathological patients find solace in music.

> Mercifully, what medication cannot achieve, music, action or art can do—*at least for the time that it lasts* ("you are the music / While the music lasts"). We have observed this, too, in many EEGs—most strikingly in two patients . . . who are highly musical. Both of these patients have grossly abnormal EEGs, with both stuporous and convulsive features. . . . But, in a way which is wonderful to see, their EEGs—like their clinical states—become entirely normal when they are playing or listening to music; only to fall back into the grossest pathology when the music stops.

This normalization sometimes occurs even if the music is played only mentally: once the music came, the EEG would instantly change; and the moment this inner performance was over, the EEG would instantly become abnormal again.[8]

In my two operas, *Passion and Resurrection* (1981) and *Inquest of Love* (1992), the healing theme is present; indeed, in the latter it is the principal theme of the work.

Passion and Resurrection, mostly written in 1980, is a setting of medieval Benedictine liturgical dramas rendered into English. It divides into two halves. The Passion is austere, chantlike, masculine in voice, and often violent. Low brass and percussion dominate. The Resurrection, on a slightly later and more poetically florid text, is more lyrical, feminine in voice (featuring the three Marys and female chorus, no more soldiers or high priests), and dominated by violin soli and trumpet. Jesus himself unites the two worlds, masculine and feminine, yin and yang, the two musics. As he sings he is always surrounded by a halo of higher harmonics or lyrical violin melodies. He sings slowly and with deep majesty, in contrast to the violent conflicts surrounding him.

It took me a long time to compose the new world of the Resurrection that he brings about. Eventually I lit on the idea of symmetrical harmony around a central axis, a floating, weaving world freed from the dark gravity of bass-oriented music— a gravity that has dominated the West since it became obsessed with individuality and its passions, signaled in the birth of the figured bass and early opera. This axial feeling became my preferred technique of harmony for many years afterward. In trying to achieve a medieval directness, I supplied all the characters with a spectrum that moved above their lines in parallel, composed of from one to twelve partials according to the dullness or brilliance of the halo I imagined them to have. The simplicity or complexity of their characters determined the limitations of the pitch repertoire they used (Peter, for example, though in some ways simple, has a largish repertoire), and characters who are in harmony with each other have many pitches in common, as opposed to characters in conflict, who have contrasting chant pitches. Jesus has the most elaborate halo and the most pitches.

Jesus, for me, heals the rift between post-Renaissance individuality and spiritual community. Modern man—philosophers and scientists, scrutinizing and proudly independent—is brought back by Jesus to the fold of unity and into a higher social order, not with an unquestioning obedience as in medieval Christianity, but with a freely chosen integrated consciousness, which contains divergence and is beyond opposites. He also restores femininity to masculinity.

The second opera, *Inquest of Love,* was written for thirteen singers, male chorus, full orchestra, and electronics. My initial idea was a sound of the sort only electronics can produce, a long, static sound in which one could live. One could explore it with one's ear like a space, now listening to higher elements, now to lower: it seemed to be all around. What I have read and sensed about life after death seemed remarkably similar to living in this music, to being music. It was pure, vibrant, flowing color emotion with no discourse or argument to distract from its essence; a sense of being: swimming in feeling, more or less refined.

I had been noting down ideas for about twenty-five years; I then wrote the libretto, a strange story of weddings, murders, and the quest for understanding, healing, and forgiveness in the afterlife. So the initial impulse was healing and unitive, and then I devised a scenario of human suffering for it to work on. An elder sister is pushed out to the periphery by her younger sister, who tries to marry the elder sister's boyfriend. The displaced sister takes the ultimate revenge: she shoots her sister, her boyfriend, and herself. It is the center/periphery conflict. But the "quest" of the title, the desire for love, always underlies the drama, even in the most violent of moments. The nature of suffering is being revealed. Once the characters realize, through angelic guidance, how they brought about the tragedy, once they perceive how they diminished and marginalized each other, once they feel another's pain as truly their own, truly connected to themselves, only then will they achieve liberation from suffering and experience the unity of love.

The spirit guides who attend the characters after death live in a sound world that is largely electronic. Their music—Philia's particularly—is based around a static harmonic series on B♭, with gentle timbre. Peaceful and timeless, it scarcely ever changes.

In the example below, Ann, the younger sister, is singing of her loneliness and isolation after death as she tries unsuccessfully to speak to her (still living) fiancé and is confused as to why everybody is looking at her dead, shed body, "my empty image on the ground." In answer to her lonely cry for help, the three guides appear and explain where she is: "It is not darkness here. Nor death. But a changing: a beat of time, in what is timeless. A breath of movement, in what is ever still."

CD 22: *Inquest of Love,* act 1

This healing action can be seen as well in the intense, raw suffering of the fiancé, John, as he begins to remember the pain he caused the elder sister by deserting her, to which Philia urges: "You can make good what you have done. It can be resolved. First know the pain that you have caused: then your healing has begun."

CD 23: *Inquest of Love,* act 2

The couple has to descend into dark, terrifying regions—a desolate subterranean landscape—to find the lost sister who resorted to murder at their wedding. The psychopomp (guide to the afterlife) whispers directions:

CD 24: *Inquest of Love,* act 2

I found it extremely difficult to compose some of the music of suffering, but David Rudkin, who helped make the libretto, and helped make the opera work for the theater, urged me to face the consequences of what I had written, to descend completely into the katabasis of despair and evade nothing. I even composed a howl of pain—"Why?" the male protagonist screams out after the senseless murder of his fiancée. It is sampled, looped, and played back over and over, often very softly, so that the tissue of blending orchestral timbre can be woven out of the quality of pain.

The movement of this and hundreds of other electronically produced or reproduced sounds in the space of the theater in a way underscores an important aspect of opera: we see people living and moving and having their being in sound; we see people-as-music. And in experiencing opera, we ourselves enter into their musical living, by identifying with them. If the music surrounds us, projected by speaker systems, this idea gains reinforcement: we are living, moving, "swimming" *in* the music.

Inquest of Love can be taken on many levels: mythological, psychoanalytical, spiritual, and so on. One that I subsequently realize lent the idea considerable power is the perinatal. The word, used by the psychotherapist Stanislav Grof, means "to do with birth." In his work (using LSD inter alia), Grof not only vividly confirmed Freud's map of regressional territory, but he took the notion even further, going back with his patients to their memories of their birth. His research in this area was considerable, and seemed in patient after patient to expose a sort of Jungian archetype of shattering power. The unity of the mother's womb was interrupted by a separation within that unity. This was followed by a desperate struggle for survival as the self, journeying along the birth canal, felt squeezed by the contractions. Devastation and annihilation ensued, to be succeeded quite suddenly by a release and a sense of freedom. Each of these biological stages could be and often was amplified into mythical, infernal, or mystical structures of great elaboration and, for the patient, overwhelming emotional and spiritual catharsis. Grof's cures were far more dramatic and effective than anybody else's; as Richard Tarnas puts it, he uncovered "a pivot that linked the biological and the archetypal, the Freudian and the Jungian, the biographical and the collective, the personal and the transpersonal, body and spirit."[9] Not only are the mind's processes archetypal, but *nature's* are too; self and object, mind and matter, share a common ontology. They are not two.

The plot of *Inquest of Love* closely reflects the perinatal archetype: the couple's wedding-day joy, the sudden severance of the murder, the struggle in "hell" to resolve unbearable conflicts, and the sudden release, with subsequent *heiros gamos* (sacred marriage) and blissful wholeness tinged by the task of starting again in the real world.

Yet dualities die hard. Returning to the holistic and transcendent quality of electronic music, I am still struck by one particular duality.[10] Recently I dreamed I could fly, and I even held fragments of ceiling in my hand to prove overwhelmingly to people it was possible, in fact easy, to defy the laws of physics. Then I awoke, and reluctantly saw I could convince no one. I have this dream often. Perhaps on this occasion it was prompted by a TV program I'd seen the evening before in which Robert Jahn, former dean of engineering at Princeton University, discussed what in his opinion was "incontrovertible evidence" for the influence of mind over matter. He was forced to resign his position and has since been shunned by many of his colleagues, some of whom spoke on the program.

My recurrent dream is often triggered by such things. Alternatively, during the day I may have an experience carrying a strong sense of the mystical or numinous or even magical, and this provokes the dream during the night. Flying seems to be a symbol for another reality about which in some obscure part of me I am totally convinced, but which is extremely difficult to communicate to others. Almost more important than the "fact" of flying is that as I wake I invariably undergo a shock at the precise moment I realize that what seemed so clearly true is "actually" not true at all. Perhaps my unhappiness over having to keep these vivid metaphysical experiences to myself alone is what drives me to communicate, to compose, and, more specifically, is what causes me to turn to electronics as a medium. Electronics are the desperate peace-broker on the battlefield where the rational self and the suppressed experiencer of a forbidden other reality fight it out.

With electronics it is common to make sounds that have no, or only vestigial, traces of human instrumental performance. No person can be envisaged blowing, hitting, or scraping anything. They are sounds of mysterious provenance.

If the speaker system is cunningly devised, the sounds, moreover, will seem to come from nowhere and float invisibly around the hall like immaterial forms. They may be pure timbre-structure, where the color itself constitutes the form. The inner nature of the sound (timbre) is what gives the music outer, factual shape. There is no distinction between inner and outer really; it is like a Möbius strip, a twisted circle of paper, which, if you were a spider walking along its path, would take you imperceptibly from the inner to the outer surface and back again.

Here is a beautifully pure example of such art, John Chowning's *Stria* for tape:

CD 25: *Stria*

Stria is a spectral piece without *objets sonores:* everything is flowing, weaving, according to inharmonic intervals and proportions. Perhaps one could describe it as one ever-changing spectrum, or thousands of spectra with blurred outlines, interfering and sometimes beating with each other in a subtle play of *accelerando* and *ritardando*. The Many and the One.

When such sounds are intermingled with recognizably human sounds, the sounds of instruments or voice, interesting things can happen, especially if it's hard to tell where one starts and the other leaves off. The implication is that they belong to the same world, not different worlds. The dreamworld in which one can fly is not a different world from the one in which we know it's physically impossible to fly. Two modes of consciousness are united.

To illustrate this, here is a process from my work for tape, live electronics, voice, and instruments called *One Evening*. A previous example contained some of the first movement; now here is a passage in the second movement where a high, colored sound on tape, a continuum, is gradually slowed down and *revealed* to be a rhythmic cell played on a recorded tabla.

CD 26: *One Evening,* second movement

The timeless radiant world of shimmering white color, lit from within, is thus seen in fact to be composed of dance rhythms, body music. This "revealing" or explication of what was implicate is as fundamental to classical music—its middleground figures that become foreground figures, for example, or its little-noticed "accompanimental" material that becomes a theme through sudden placement in the limelight—as it is fundamental to mystical experience, as in the "form-luminescence" breathing oscillations described earlier. Sudden perceptions of unity, or conversely, of the components of what we previously perceived as a unity, are the essence both of music and of spiritual perception. The words for that passage from *One Evening* were adapted from just such a spiritual perception, which was recorded in a letter to a friend by Rabindranath Tagore:

> As I was watching it (the sunrise), suddenly . . . a veil seemed to be lifted from my eyes. I found the world wrapt in inexpressible glory with its waves of joy and beauty bursting and breaking on all sides. The thick cloud of sorrow that lay on my heart in many folds was pierced through and through by the light of the world, which was everywhere radiant . . .
>
> There was nothing and no one whom I did not love at that moment. . . . I stood on the veranda and watched the coolies as they tramped down the road. Their movements, their forms, their countenances seemed strangely wonderful to me, as if they were all moving like waves in the great ocean of the world. . . . I seemed to witness, in the wholeness of my vision, the movements of the body of all humanity, and to feel the beat of the music and the rhythm of a mystic dance.[11]

A second example from *One Evening* shows the process reversed: body music flies up to the pure continuum, from the physical to the metaphysical, from sounds obviously produced by human action to sounds with no direct human source. And yet, of course, one hears the connection. It is the duality contained in unity. But this example also, like the Möbius strip, goes further, returning back to where it started—with corporeal rhythm. The acceleration continues until the first, accented note of each rhythmic cell begins to occur so fast that it rises into the frequency range. This begins to happen at around sixteen cycles per second. So a deep note, colored by the higher frequencies above it of the quicker notes in the original rhythmic cell, begins to rise up in a glissando. It stops at the pitch-point where the rhythmic cells have been occurring, and the rhythm starts over again. So the unity of rhythm, pitch, and color, as Stockhausen long ago observed, is shown to be, like the rest of the universe, all a matter of tempo, of speed, of energy.

CD 27: *One Evening,* fourth movement

The unifying of things I feel are contradictory, or ambiguously separate at least, has been a constant theme of my electronic music, live and taped. *Mortuos Plango, Vivos Voco* is a tape work built on the voice of my chorister son and that of the great tenor bell at Winchester Cathedral. I used to listen enthralled to the mingled sounds of the choir rehearsing in the vast cathedral while far above the bells were pealing. This almost chaotic unity made me want to explore a seamless movement from bell to boy in my piece, something possible in 1980 in Europe only with the computer of IRCAM. By creating computer simulations of both bell and boy I was able to interpolate between one set of digital numbers and another and so find a unified world in which both were present simultaneously.

CD 28: "Sketch" for *Mortuos Plango, Vivos Voco*

Here is the moment in the piece where that boy-bell oscillation occurs. You hear the boys later pointing out the upper partials of the bell in their chords: the whole piece is like the unfolding in time of what is in fact one moment, the timbre of the bell. The vertical become horizontal—spectral form.

CD 29: *Mortuos Plango, Vivos Voco*

The speed at which the bell tolls and at which the boy chants is determined by the principle of the equivalence of tempo and frequency. If the pitch is down an octave, the tolling tempo is twice as slow, the section twice as long; and corresponding ratios apply for all other intervals of frequency. Each of the eight sections is based on one partial of the spectrum (establishing global unity between sections), and this partial observes the above ratios, thus unifying pitch, tempo, and duration within each section. In a well-projected performance the audience should feel that at times the bell surrounds them, with different partials sounding in different speakers (unification of space), whereas the boy is mobile, flying like a free spirit. The "dead" bell is the *mortuos*, the "living" boy the *vivos*. They are one.

Rituals are for binding together contrasted personalities. In a later IRCAM tape piece, *Ritual Melodies*, I made, together with Jan Vandenheede, melodies from computer simulations of traditional instruments. Each melody achieved smooth changes of color by oscillating between two instruments, so again, one could scarcely tell where one ended and the other started. The world of numbers unified them: not just in wave form, but in their behavior in time, how they moved from note to note, how they vibrated, how much noise they embodied, and so on. Two such sturdily independent personalities as the shakuhachi and the Indian oboe, not designed like our instruments to blend in orchestras, had their inner structures converted into each other. So the individuated world is seen as one unitive world.

Here's one such melody:

CD 30: *Ritual Melodies,* melody A

And here's another, hybridizing Indian oboe and Tibetan temple bowl:

CD 31: *Ritual Melodies,* melody B

Ritual Melodies takes the idea of ambiguity into other musical areas as well. For instance, each of these well-formed melodies (eight in all) can form a composite melody with its neighbor: a busier melody in which the computer precisely slots the moving bits of one melody into the static or silent bits of the other. That way, the composite melodies, which I went to great trouble to endow with good form in themselves, were at once ambiguous yet unified.

Here is the composite of the two previous examples; one, as you heard, had melismata, the other, dotted rhythms.

CD 32: *Ritual Melodies,* melody AB

In the work as a whole, a correspondence holds between the timbres of the instruments, which of course are all constituted in the normal harmonic series (except the temple bowl), and the melodic notes they play, which are all drawn from a normal harmonic series as well. The fundamental of this series is actually the G just off the bottom of the piano, but I only use the higher partials, from the sixth to the fortieth. So the acoustic structure (of the notes) is the same as the melodic structure (of the piece). The microcosm corresponds to the macrocosm.

Also, the melodies are prolonged into a "cloud" by reverberation, so the harmonic series sounds sometimes as a chord, sometimes as a timbre. We move between discourse and color, as in *Madonna of Winter and Spring* (see chapter 2). Here is a passage that leads from "clouds"—reverberated bits of melody—to melodies:

CD 33: *Ritual Melodies*

The art of *live* electronics highlights the unity of ambiguity still further. When electronics are performed in real time like instruments and combined with instruments or voices, the two worlds merge in a theater of transformations and legerdemain. No one listening knows exactly what is instrumental and what is electronic anymore. Legerdemain deceives the audience as in a magic show. When they lack connection to the familiar instrumental world, electronics can be overwhelmingly alien— other, inhuman, inadmissible, dismissable (like the notion of flying in a rational world). When electronics are seamlessly connected to the physical, solid instrumental world, however, an expansion of the admissible takes place and the "irrational" world is made to belong. If electronic sounds are completely separate from traditional instruments, they may as well be on the moon: there can be no measurement of interval and consequently no music.

My live electronic works incorporate several degrees of "liveness." Some sounds are created for an electronic instrument that allows fluent movement, just as a cellist creates fluid sounds within the physical parameters of the cello. In the electronic case the parameters are more or less compositorially determined: the sounds are "notelike," limited but playable in complex configurations. At the other extreme one finds sounds that are considerably more fixed; usually longer in duration, more like a "passage" than a "note"; and at a higher level of structure, molecular rather than atomic. These creations typically take many days or even weeks of studio work to perfect. If they extend beyond a certain length they begin to correspond to the non–real time notion of "tape," with its connotations of performer slavery (for their time cannot be changed). In between these two extremes can be found every imaginable degree of liveness, every level of fixity. Because all these sounds are presented through the same loudspeakers, proliferating and often simultaneously, the listener has little chance of knowing where instrumentality stops and where fixed object-like "tape" music starts.

Only with great familiarity will it become clear that whereas some sounds are fluid and spontaneously change from performance to performance, others remain the same. And yet the duality, too, is fascinating. One may hear the fixed sounds in a new way from performance to performance as they are rearticulated by their shifting context (just as the river one stood in yesterday is different from the one entered today). If performing styles change in seventy years' time, it would be interesting to see how the "unchanging" recorded passages work with and influence new slants of interpretation. By the same token, synthesizers become quite rapidly obsolete, and updating their role in a piece may necessarily involve changing the sound— though the digitally sampled sounds themselves should be able to pass unscathed from century to century.

Certainly my most ambitious attempt in this area has been the opera *Inquest of Love* (see above and CD extracts 22–24). For two hours the synthesizers, tapes, and live electronic treatments of the orchestra, and to a lesser extent the singers, weave in and out of the electronic and instrumental worlds, with the border between them completely blurred. The point is to show the unity of normal reality and a spiritual world, of life

and death, of physics and metaphysics. To perceive this connection is to be aware in the world; it is also the nature of art.
Both realities, normal and spiritual, are enigmatic, and to
embrace them is to be "liberated into tension," to realize a
state of calm that is vibrant rather than empty. Recall George
Steiner's Saturday, between Good Friday and Easter Sunday:
we inhabit an empty world pregnant with extraordinary hints
and glimpses. With patience the silence will perhaps yield
something quite new.

4

Stasis and Silence

Art is often linked to the transcendent, for it seems to speak of things that cannot be expressed any other way. According to the *Oxford English Dictionary,* the word *transcendent* signifies that which lies beyond the range or grasp of human experience, reason, or belief. In finding art to be linked to the transcendent, then, I am experiencing something that cannot be experienced, because it is beyond experience.

If art cannot reveal the transcendent, perhaps it does something weaker, like intimate or suggest the transcendent (this is close to Kant's account of aesthetic ideas). But, as T. J. Diffey points out, you have to know what the transcendent actually is before you can say with any authority that art is suggesting it.[1] And if we don't experience the transcendent, we can't very well know it.

All we can do, in other words, is question whether it is true that the transcendent is in fact beyond our experience. If we accept the dictionary definition, although we would be in agreement with the majority of post-Enlightenment thinkers in the West, we would be discounting the evidence of most Eastern philosophers and any who claim to have had mystical experiences. It seems that either the word is wrongly defined or else *transcendent* is the wrong word to use in our discussion, and *mystical* might be more appropriate.

Very roughly, there are two main types of mystical or transcendental experience. The first is a well-documented event, to be found, for example, in William James's *The Varieties of Religious Experience,*[2] in the Alister Hardy Research Center collection in Oxford, which houses hundreds of personal accounts (apparently about 30 percent of English people have had some sort of mystical experience), and in many autobiographies and poems. It is the sudden, transforming opening to a new dimension—very emotional, very powerful. Many who experience it do so only once in a lifetime, but they regard it as the most important moment of their lives.

The other type of experience is almost the opposite: it is to become very still. Techniques of meditation are often formulated to achieve this descent into stillness, as the monkeylike mind ceases its restless activity and plunges into nothingness. The mind, though fully awake, is conscious of nothing. This sort of transcendence takes years of practice to achieve for anything more than a second or two. The curious thing is that you can't "know" anything about this state: it is a blank. But you know, when you come out of it, as I have done thousands of times, that you have been there; you have a great sense of calmness and lightness and you are full of creative ideas, solutions to problems, and various vivid, clear mental notions. It is said to be the womb of all creativity.

Music seems to deal with these borderlands. Although it is true to say you cannot "know" transcendence, in that it is beyond knowledge, it is not true to say you cannot experience it. In other words, it is a different type of experience from that of which the dictionary speaks: it is a state of consciousness—the ontological dimension again, subtly different from the normal idea of knowing something. Knowing and being are collapsed into one. But if you travel the pathway to and from this "other thing," you learn to recognize the borderlands, the surroundings in which it exists, very well. To achieve transcendence one must become very still; and having touched it, one comes in touch with the source of creativity—imagination at its most vivid, its most real.

So there we have the two contrasting elements we've talked of so often before in reference to music's ambiguity: stillness and moving vividness, emptiness and fullness, unity and variety, the One and the Many. Stillness, in "spiritual" music, could be seen as a vessel for energy. Stillness permeates energy; energy is shot through with stillness. In tantric Buddhism, which embodies perhaps the most profound of Shakyamuni's teachings, this power is related to the union of emptiness and bliss.

Although I believe this "stillness" can be found in all great music, there are occasions when composers make us especially aware of its presence. Certain forms, such as classical variations, passacaglias, and chaconnes, foreground the element of repetition strongly, yet display variety and transformative ingenuity as necessary elements as well.

Minimalism might be cited as an extreme example of repetition, although in its "purest" form, where there is very little variety, the ambiguity of the One and the Many is weakened. In the less successful manifestations of this style, as a result, the overall oneness, the total form, is not very strong; it is repetition without unification. Unification needs contrasts with which to articulate itself. On the other hand, it can be relatively easy to become one with the music at a very basic level where a trancelike state may be induced, as occurs with certain dance, pop, and rock music; this level is an important ingredient of crossover style, where rock meets classical, often used by minimalism. In all these music types, however, the listener is probably less conscious of unity than would be the case with materially more complex works.

Of course, the exploration of "vertical-time" music, in which any passage, any gesture, can only be sensibly related "upward" to the *whole* form,[3] is one of the great adventures of the 1960s and 1970s and, indeed, one of the greatest revolutions in music of the twentieth century. If, for example, linear time is 1,2,3, then vertical time is some disordering, like

2,1,3—it can be understood only when viewed as a complete entity, as a global relation of equal steps whose order *in time* is unimportant. In that particular aesthetic, disruptive formal surprises would certainly be regarded as damaging to the central aims, because the *line* of linear time is not there, so cannot meaningfully be broken into.

A good illustration of the mainstream use of repetition (as *one* element in a complex process) to achieve an expressive stillness behind energy—in this case, a portrait of obsession—is the passacaglia in act 2 of Britten's *Death in Venice* (see example 21). This opera is a profound commentary on the dangerous, even threatening, relationship of music to the semantic world. Britten transposes Thomas Mann's Tadzio into a wordless music, which, at its dark edge, spreads into an obsessive music, one that questions all the master-writer Aschenbach's carefully built up world order (and, as it were, "word" order). The passacaglia contains thirty-four repetitions in the bass of the cell connected with the cholera, combined with motives associated with Tadzio's Polish family. During the eight repetitions of this bass-cell based on F, Aschenbach sings, "Yet I am driven on."

When Richard Strauss played the score of *Salome* on the piano to his eighty-three-year-old father, the old man complained of its restlessness, which he memorably compared to having an insect crawling around inside one's clothes. This astonishingly inventive score, by a man who detested religion, has at its climax an extraordinary pedal device whose effect is not merely sensational, exciting, morbid, erotic, or any of the other usual descriptions of Salome, but, I would say, profound. It is profound because it is a moment of fulfillment—perverted fulfillment perhaps, yet certainly the achievement of a goal. It is the moment the whole story leads to, when the head of John the Baptist (Jokanaan) is presented to Salome on a silver platter. A huge black arm, the arm of the Executioner, comes forth from the dungeon bearing the gruesome object. Salome sings "Ah! Du wolltest mich nicht deinen Mund küssen lassen, Jokanaan! Wohl ich werde ihn jetzt küssen!" (Ah! Thou wouldst not let me kiss thy mouth, Jokanaan! Well, I will kiss it now!).

Strauss gives Salome soaring lines over a rich web of themes and a tonic pedal C♯ (see example 22). The effect of this tonic pedal (and I emphasize *tonic*) after so much restless harmony is to broaden things out into a new perspective. Time is suddenly larger in its span. It is as if the pedal has been there secretly all along—Salome has always known she would kiss Jokanaan's mouth, and it was her real nature to do this across the borderland of death. I hear something transcending time at this point, even though the ecstasy of a murderess has nothing obviously to do with the spiritual.

My words introducing Salome's apotheosis were personal and quite possibly inadequate. However one interprets the pedal, we can probably agree that Strauss's use of it in an exceptionally restless ninety minutes is a means of pointing to the stillness, the stasis, that can be found in even the most excited, aroused art, which elevates it to the monumental: a statement of enduring, eternal values, beyond time.

There can be little doubt that something like this was in Brahms's mind when, in the *Deutsches Requiem,* he described what it means to live in the hand of God. After the lamentations of "Behold thou hast made my days a few handbreadths, and my lifetime is as nothing in thy sight" we come to "But the souls of the righteous are in the hand of God, and there shall no torment touch them." Brahms sets this over a tonic D pedal. (Dominant pedals have a completely different dynamic in most tonal music, of course; they do not suggest the meaning *of* underlying the whole piece, being always there.) The souls of the righteous sing a busy, joyful fugue while the hand of God holds them from below—again, in a world beyond time (see example 23).

The ultimate in tonic pedals must belong to North Indian music, though the tanpura's drone dates only from about the seventeenth century (I suspect it was incorporated from other, more ancient music, at that time). I need hardly expand on the spiritual intensity, the longing for God and transcendence, associated with such music, which, in Ghandharva Veda, one of the ancient Vedic pathways, is the way to divine wisdom. "Out of the complex fabric of subtle sound arose the concept of *Pranava, Omkara,* as the source of all sound. Sound and life being inseparable, the former was identified with god, . . . the latter with life. . . . Herein lay the unity of spirit and matter."[4]

Let us leave the stasis of pedals, where the Many and the One are pointed up separately (the static in the bass, the mobile in the upper parts), and turn to modality, where the One permeates the Many *without* being separated from it. A mode is a scale with which the music actively operates. A mode ceases to be a mode when it includes all twelve semitones (presuming, that is, that we are talking about pitch classes, which are the same in each octave, and not including microtones). An eleven-tones-per-octave mode is the densest possible; after that we reach the chromatic plenum, which cannot be characterized as having a distinctive set of possibilities.

The thinnest mode, at the other end, occurs just before the scale becomes a chord of three or four notes. We could, of course, think of a diminished seventh chord as a mode, but we probably wouldn't because it is too simple to allow music a global repertoire to move around in; generally, therefore, we think of it as a local musical element. A five-part chord, however, can flip over conceptually and be either a chord or a mode: hence the ubiquitous pentatonic modes. Conceptually, they live on the ambiguous edge, complex enough to allow for extended musical development, simple enough to give an impression of stasis, of not developing—an impression of living in the hand of God, which is precisely the purpose of Gregorian chant, for which pentatonicism often forms a backbone.

Before coming to the pentatonic proper, we should note the citation, in works by composers ranging from Beethoven to Arvo Pärt, of the old church modes. Referring to an age of faith in itself conveys a spiritual message, of course; but in the *Heiliger Dankgesang* of Beethoven's Quartet op. 132, and even more in most of Pärt's music, the lengthy stasis, especially the prolongation of flattened sevenths, creates a strong sense of undisturbed timelessness. Further emphasized by extremely minor variation, great length, and pervasive silence, a work like Pärt's *Passio Domini nostri secundum Iohannem* (1982) itself comes very close to mystical practice. Pärt clips off each phrase just before it becomes expressive, subjective (see example 24). After each completed gesture he gives us space to stand back and contemplate it as an object without rushing us on to the next thing. "Through-flow" of a developing emotion is curtailed.

The same extreme negation of self-expression is found in John Tavener's use of Orthodox chant, both as a reference (to give the message) and as a stasis (to convey timelessness and unitive consciousness). The icon is the model, with its "elimination of the author" and its formal stillness. Tavener believes that the composer must have a strong consciousness of the drone, or traditional *ison*, representing eternity, though he may dance in and out of it. See example 25 for part of a movement of *Ikon of Light* (1983), setting the Trisagion, a much-used Orthodox prayer.

Both Pärt and Tavener are concerned with prayer, which, perhaps rightly, they consider more important than music. It is a balancing act between utter selflessness, on the one hand, and expression that is a *renewal* of tradition, on the other. Music that is so stripped of polyphonic and harmonic elaboration that it takes second place to the symbolic significance may prove inaccessible to those unsympathetic to that significance; in others, however, such music can often trigger powerful spiritual experiences.

When a mode divides the octave symmetrically, it ceases to have the goal orientation of the diatonic system and becomes a musical expression of suspension in space. Here music is not symbolizing; it is itself a form of prayer, a means for experiencing unity. It is not a code for pointing *to* something; rather, it seems to have an inner feeling *of* something. The best-known type of pentatonic mode, which divides the octave symmetrically into tone, minor third, tone, minor third, tone, is a good example (see example 26).

Any of the notes in this example could plausibly form a bass, a finishing prioritized, note. It floats in space without gravity, more like an abstract painting than one with ground and sky. It seems to go back in time long before anybody thought of bass domination, whether of the figured sort or of the instrumental sort. Prebaroque music in most cultures seems to be rather lacking in powerful bass instruments. Only the advent of mechanical means, with few exceptions, achieved the necessary energy for our descent into loud, low sound, with the aid of organs, and now amplification and synthesizers.

When tonality began to develop, around 1600, so did consciousness of the harmonic series, which has as its foundation the octave. Octaves in the bass developed concurrently with tonality. Only after the liberating innovation of atonality, when the bass once again became unimportant, or at least only semi-functional, could composers go back to the bass with clean hands (and fresh minds) and rediscover the harmonic series in the form of spectralism.

However, it's not that line of development I want to follow now, since it was discussed earlier. The symmetrical (bassless) pentatonic mode surfaces briefly with the turn to the Romantic new world of Schubert, subtle but unmistakable: in "Des Baches Wiegenlied" (the final song of *Die schöne Müllerin*—a timeless lullaby-in-death), for instance, or in "Die Krähe" from *Winterreise*, at the words *Krähe, wunderliches Tier*—one of the most sublime moments in all Schubert. It returns at crucial points in recent music as well. A case in point is *Le martyre de Saint Sébastien*, in which Debussy uses this mode for the more spiritual moments of D'Annunzio's text. Another is Mahler's *Das Lied von der Erde* and the first subject of his Ninth Symphony, first movement. It seems very likely that Mahler had heard Chinese music on a wax cylinder—obviously the high tenor in *Das Lied* derives from it, but the pentatonicism that so achingly pervades these settings of old Chinese texts, as adapted by Judith Gautier and Hans Bethge, is both an echo of oriental holism and a limitation of tonal richness, such that "unity" is forced upon our attention.

The famous ending of *Das Lied* on the contralto's D—supertonic in tonal terms, merely suspended in pentatonic terms (mirrored in the ending on the same degree of the scale in the lower register in the Ninth, first movement)—is all the more poignant because the music moves to it so gradually as, one by one, all the nonpentatonic pitches are stripped away. The last to go is the minor third (E♭), which, in its lingering insistence, seems an archetype of the sadness of parting. Yet the Romantic weltanschauung does not hold Mahler, and he ultimately progresses to the Buddhist attainment of nonattachment, in the end relinquishing this note too. All attachments, cravings, and illusions are peeled away to reveal Pure Mind. It exists, timeless, eternal, underneath the entire work: a dissolution into what was always there. We hear the connection.

A similar transition occurs at the end of Schoenberg's *Verklärte Nacht*. Here again, the text behind the sextet expresses suffering and its release. The shadowy couple portrayed in Dehmel's poem walk at night in anguish, and at the end find reconciliation by merging their identities with the glorious transfiguration of light, the moonlight that pervades all. Out of extreme chromaticism comes a pentatonicism (tinged and complex, but easily recognizable) based on the added sixth.

Berg likewise ended his Violin Concerto by twisting his serial system so that it could accommodate not only his Schoenberg-father but also his other musical father, Mahler. The final movement graphically portrays the "death of an angel"—the young Manon Gropius—and sings her requiem-transfiguration with variations on Bach's chorale "Es ist genug." These phrases become ever more unworldly as the violin-soul rises higher, mingling in unison with the orchestral violins, dissolving into unity, and finally separating at the end, to rest atop a pentatonic added sixth (see example 27).

The clearest example of the period is perhaps Fauré's "In Paradisum" from the *Requiem* (see example 28); there is no mere suggestion of timeless suspension here: it is on the surface.

I have developed the idea of symmetrical pentatonicism in several of my works—for instance, by extending the alternation of tone and minor third so that it does not repeat in each octave but repeats only after five octaves, having encompassed all twelve pitch classes en route (see example 29). This kind of mode, or harmonic field, is static both in its local, small-scale symmetry and overall (though the complexity of the whole is of course greater).

I use it to suggest peacefulness, to intimate the peace that passes all understanding; it is complex enough, moreover, not to threaten the global atonal discourse with incongruous tonal references. In the next example it floats up, disappears as the high sounds descend, and then reasserts itself naturally to make a dying fade.

CD 34: *Song Offerings,* third movement

Most of the harmonic fields I use have four properties: they divide a certain span of roughly an octave or double octave symmetrically; they are inversional around a governing axis for the piece; they are made of only two or three intervals; and they are atonal within about two octaves' span. As harmonic fields, in addition, they can remain in place for anything between a second and ten minutes and thus have the ability to achieve large-scale stasis. They can also act like Schenkerian prolongation or even background (*Hintergrund*), returning at the end of the piece. In short, they are indistinguishable from modes.

The symmetrical modes that Messiaen uses, in contrast, are confined to a single octave; hence, they repeat in each octave. He regarded the limited transposition that could be applied to such pitch-class modes before they duplicated themselves as indicative of their static quality. They pervade space, like Swedenborg's angels, knowing no direction except everywhere.

Books have been written about the profoundly spiritual genius of Messiaen's concept of time. Indeed, he himself wrote seven volumes on rhythm (apart from the early *Technique de mon langage musical*), which were published only posthumously.[5] Suffice it to say here that in the *Technique* he expounds his belief that nonretrogradable rhythms—palindromes that repeat backward what we have just heard forward—compress time into a nondirectional time capsule, using the iconography of eternity. In a work like "Soixante-quatre durées" from his

Livre d'orgue, all eleven and a half minutes are one palindrome, a retrograde canon using a symmetrical series of sixty-four durations once each. Such an expansion of the earlier quite perceptible phrase-shaping to something only a superconsciousness could perceive is a gesture toward the ineffable— the color-flow of time as seen from above, from the position of transcendence. Against this monumental, almost static picture Messiaen places Blackbird, Great Tit, Great Spotted Woodpecker, and other creatures presumably as exclusively concerned with the "now" as the other plane is exclusively concerned with the eternal (see example 30).

Webern, another absolutist, whose works are as superhumanly short as Messiaen's are superhumanly long, shares also a love of palindromes and symmetrical structures poised directionless in space, only in his case they are dodecaphonic rather than modal. Strict serial technique has at its heart an emphasis on canceling the arrow of time and direction in space, with its retrogrades and inversions of the series, respectively. Despite some metaphysical remarks by Schoenberg, for whom prayer became paramount and pure order without color seemed an inexpressible ideal—as inexpressible as the apprehension of God, despite hints like the Burning Bush and Moses' utterances in *Moses und Aron*—it was Webern's music that drew out the floating, timeless quality of serialism most clearly.

The First Cantata, for instance, begins with a four-part canon by retrogression (see example 31). This yields mirror symmetry in the domain of harmony and intervals. Webern, in his juxtapositions of slow chords with faster cascades, creates also rhythmic and metric mirror symmetries, which are clarified by the instrumental colors. These are complex but audible palindromes. As he put it, "Everything remains in a floating state."[6]

Perhaps the most interesting of Webern's phases is the so-called free atonal or expressionist one. The music is not only extremely brief, but it is constituted to an unprecedented degree by silence. For instance, "O sanftes Glühn der Berge" is an orchestral song written in 1913 but first performed only in 1966 after being rescued from an attic by Hans Moldenhauer.

In ten of its thirty-five bars the orchestra plays nothing, and the average number of notes per bar overall is less than two, in a slow tempo; only the voice moves, like a spirit, as the orchestra holds its breath, almost entirely *ppp*.

Webern wrote the words himself, and as in all his works from this period, the subject is the death of his mother. He used to go in the evening, he explained to Schoenberg, to sit by her grave in the mountainside cemetery and experience the silence there. He spoke also of the curious warmth of his mother's presence to him.[7] The extraordinary silence and associated feelings of presence, I believe, formed the spiritual basis of his impulse to create music.

The poem in "O sanftes Glühn" goes like this:

Oh gentle mountain radiance,
(*whispered*) now I see her again.
Oh God, so tender and beautiful,
Mother of Grace in heaven's height,
bend down, oh come once more . . .

(*very softly spoken*) You greet and bless . . .

(*sung*) The breath of evening takes the light.
I see it no more,
your beloved face.

At the precious words "You greet and bless" (*Du grüsst und segnest*) there is an unutterably soft solo muted violin playing a repeated minor ninth E/F and a tubular bell playing an E♭— distant, "sacred," and quite static. There follows not silence but a bass drum roll, "distant" cowbells, and a brief low timpani roll—sounds of nature, of space, all scarcely audible. "The breath of evening," on flute and muted trumpet fluttertongue with mandolin tremolando, rustles through the silence; there is a sighing glissando in the muted viola for "I see it no more" (*Ich seh's nicht mehr*) and, on *Dein liebes* (Your beloved) the most infinitely delicate touch of warmth on the major third at the end (see example 32). For the final *Angesicht* (face) there is only silence, leaving the unsayable merely implied (see example 33). It is hard not to feel heavy-handed after hearing such music. It is an extraordinary fact that Webern's intense spiritual experiences in that remote, silent spot influenced a fair part of the course of twentieth-century music.

In a typical meditation, thoughts become more and more refined, subtle, delicate—until they disappear into silence. Seen as the vanishing point of refinement, silence can be pregnant with meaning, carrying the process of refinement into the unknown, beyond thought.

I have tried in several works to alternate almost-silence with silence. For instance, in *Madonna of Winter and Spring* the Winter section comes after a long descent, which sinks deeper and deeper into lifelessness, hibernation. Then Winter simply stays on two adjacent notes as buried reminders of the thematic discourse stir ever more sluggishly beneath, dying down bit by bit.

CD 35: *Madonna of Winter and Spring*

In *Inner Light (2)* (1977), Kipling's strange story "They," about the ghosts of children who inhabit a remote and beautiful country house, is used as a text, which is interwoven with T. S. Eliot's *Burnt Norton,* borrowing such images as "hidden laughter of children in the foliage." The fleeting glimpses of these half-hidden presences is reflected in the music by soft scurrying fragmentations of the "rational" material, alternating with silences. The passage is then repeated as a negative, as it were, the silences having the exact lengths of the earlier sounds and vice versa. Silence is absence: absence *of* something.

CD 36: *Inner Light (2)*

In *Bhakti* (1982), too, the approach leading to the still center of the work is permeated with silence. The work began by assembling pitch-content outward from a single middle G. Having reached its fullest state, it sheds pitch-content until it arrives back at repeated Gs, but in the ninth movement they are transformed into three massive Gs explored spectrally on tape. Each movement bears at its end a quotation from the *Rig Veda,* a collection of ancient hymns in which multivalent Sanskrit words united rather than divided the world, resembling in some ways modernist poetry. The ninth has: "The quarters of the sky live on the oceans that flow out of her in all directions. The whole universe exists through the undying syllable that flows from her." Here is the approach to that movement and the beginning of the movement itself:

CD 37: *Bhakti,* end of eighth movement and beginning of ninth

Such silence-filled ideas are, of course, inherent in certain oriental traditions such as Zen Buddhism. Zen has cast its influence on figures as different as John Cage and Toru Takemitsu (see example 34). Takemitsu was working in a Western musical language, but, like a Japanese novel translated into English, his compositions contain something different. Takemitsu said he only uttered 80 percent of any idea, in what could be construed as powerful understatement; the rest is silence, the pregnancy of the unsaid, *ma. Ma,* a profoundly important concept in Japanese culture, is the silent understanding when friends are together, or when one is contemplating nature or art—when meaning is intense but nothing is expressed. For Takemitsu the "single sound" (together with silence) produced by great masters of the biwa or shakuhachi served as a model:

> A single strum of the strings or even one pluck is too complex, too complete in itself to admit any theory. Between this complex sound—so strong that it can stand alone— and that point of intense silence preceding it, called *ma,* there is a metaphysical continuity that defies analysis.
>
> . . . In its complexity and its integrity this single sound can stand alone. To the sensitive Japanese listener who appreciates this refined sound, the unique idea of *ma*— the unsounded part of this experience—has at the same time a deep, powerful and rich resonance that can stand up to the sound.
>
> . . . I wish to search out that single sound which is in itself so strong that it can confront silence. It is then that my own personal insignificance will cease to trouble me.[8]

Cage's view of silence, which was to make the ordinary special, is too complex a topic for discussion here; however, in the sense that the "author" is almost completely absent from his works (Cage claimed he did not "hear" what he wrote but wished to be "surprised," to experience the joy of the unintended) and that he was interested not in exploring the logic of sound but rather sought to liberate into being the "incalculable infinity of causes and effects"—an attitude very close to Buddhist impermanent "emptiness"—his aesthetic could be thought of as spiritual. Nevertheless, as with Marcel Duchamp's readymades, I miss in his work that which music best conveys: the near-transcendent, the delicate voice of a friend, as intangible as a wisp of smoke.

I spoke earlier about some of my own works being "closer" to me than others. I cannot define what this "me" is to which those works are close, but the ones I prepare for more deeply seem to come from some central place within my being. For these works I spend a few weeks becoming stiller, withdrawing from the world, experiencing subtler and ever more refined thoughts and feelings until finally I arrive at the core of the work—or is it the core of myself? Many other composers have given accounts of similar processes of preparation and withdrawal. (With *The Riot* I didn't prepare like this, hence my attitude to the work in the first chapter.)

Should one call this most personal of experiences spiritual? I do know that the works for which I prepare deeply are, for me, spiritual creations. If the word has a living meaning, as opposed to a parroted, formal one, then perhaps it lies in what seems deepest, most intimately part of ourselves. This "special" category is the subjective, defining one for the composer, though it has little to do with the listener.

Several writers, such as those anthologized in Godwin's historical survey *Music, Mysticism, and Magic,*[9] have written about how such experience fits into a view of the world. Indeed, all the major religions and many individuals embrace often remarkably similar musical cosmologies. Let me mention just one such person: Rudolf Steiner, an Austrian scholar and spiritual leader who worked in the first quarter of this century. Not only was he a man of discriminating intelligence, but he had the gift of clairvoyance as well. We have touched already on the problem of conveying spiritual experience in language other than music. I do not know whether Steiner's words are true in the scientific, dualist sense. I regard them as poetry, even as music: they excite me deeply and strangely, and their impact has not faded over the twenty-five years I have been acquainted with them.

He said in 1906 that meditation, or rather the more advanced state he called initiation, transforms the three states of consciousness: waking, dreaming, and deep sleep. If one becomes utterly still in waking consciousness, one's dream life transforms. One perceives a new world, one is "living and weaving in a world of colours and light." Later, one becomes capable of retaining consciousness throughout dreamless sleep:

> The colours become increasingly transparent, and the light becomes ever clearer and at the same time spiritualised. . . . Man has the sensation that he himself lives in the colour and this light, as if they do not surround him but rather he himself is colour and light. . . . Gradually, this deep stillness begins to resound spiritually, softly at first, then louder and louder. The world of colour and light is permeated with resounding tones.[10]

Steiner elaborates on how this nightly bathing in spiritual worlds (but not only bathing: *becoming* light, *becoming* sound nondualistically) reminds us what our true home is, and refreshes and consoles us. "Inspired" composers bring back from that spiritual homeland glimpses and intuitions (they do not need to be initiated to have these), which they translate into physical, instrumental, or vocal sounds. The process is unconscious unless one is clairvoyant, but it exists nevertheless: the inspired draw on it.

Steiner wrote as early as 1923 of how the single note would in future be found as rich in meaning as an entire symphony— a prophecy now coming true before our ears. This he called the spiritualization of music, the penetration of its inner nature.

Stockhausen and Giacinto Scelsi may well have been influenced by Steiner; each in his own way is both openly spiritual in purpose and obsessed with the single note, the inner sound. My last example will be from Stockhausen, the composer who articulated the idea of Moment Form, where time is no longer linear but centered in itself, the eternal "now." The work I want to discuss, however, is not primarily of this type: it is more complex, more ambiguous. It is *Inori* (Japanese for prayer, invocation, adoration) from 1974, and there is much *ma* here. *Inori,* a work for orchestra with a soloist who prays, develops both the stasis of the single pitch and the pregnancy of silence. The extraordinary originality of this work is that it makes visible what we have been talking about: the soloist is a mime artist who performs the gestures of prayer as found in various cultures. Sometimes, as in the example that follows, there is silence (or colored silence, as Stockhausen calls soft reverberations and lingering echoes) during which we see the conductor still beating the progress of the time structure and the mime continuing the choreography. At such points we almost feel we can hear a hidden music, one too subtle for instruments. The silence is full to bursting. The part of the mime is strictly integrated to the quasi-serial structure of the work's overriding formula. Prayer is "made visible" by a scale of thirteen gestures specific to prayer, plus four extra gestures. These correspond to the orchestral timbres. Each gesture can be performed with one of sixty degrees of intensity (closed–open), corresponding to sixty degrees of orchestral loudness. The mime signals the register of the pitches by sitting, kneeling, or standing when performing the prayer movements. And of course they are enacted in equivalent rhythms and tempi. So we see a deeply structural counterpoint (not a slavish one-to-one choreography) to the musical discourse. It is as if prayer—spiritual experience itself—has become music. From discourse becoming one with spirit we have turned full circle: spirit has here become one with discourse.

If you succeeded in "becoming" the sounds in the example

in chapter 1, as Stockhausen recommended, here you must try
to become the silences as well:

**CD 38: Stockhausen, *Inori*, sections III (Echo), IV (Pause),
and the beginning of V (Genesis)**

Music's connection with spirituality *can* be thought of as
music acting as a trigger for the spiritual experience. Spirituality in this view resides in subjects, not objects; in people, not
music. The music may be explicitly spiritual (a mass for example) or not, but the experience is necessarily subjective, and
anybody is free to find any music spiritual, however likely or
unlikely it may seem. As Wittgenstein pointed out, such an
instrumentalist view trivializes art by making it *merely* a
means to the desired end, so if a more efficacious means of
attaining the end (drugs, for instance) became available, art
would be redundant, its value exhausted and discarded.[11]

But I have also proposed, even favored, another view, a view
that is beyond the subject/object duality altogether. It is a view
incompatible with the current fashion in the science of consciousness, namely, the reduction of consciousness to neurons,
of humans to zombies.[12] It still needs us to lend a willing ear,
but if the process works, it transcends the subjective, it even
transcends our "core," just as it transcends duality, and we can
say—as we can say that we and the music are one—that music
is by its very nature spiritual or that we *and* the music are spiritual. Fundamentally, and following tradition, the "spiritual" is
the experience of *unity*.[13] The implications of such experience
are enormous: they reach right across to Buddha's "I show you
suffering and I show you the release from suffering." Where
there is unity, there is compassion: sympathy and solidarity
with suffering. In our arid, rigid, confrontational, dualistic age
we need this experience of music as an urgent necessity; without such values we will die as a civilization.

In the Buddhist (particularly Tibetan) worldview the concept of unity—"pure mind"—transcends death, as of course it
must if it is indeed beyond time. The restlessness that is our
karma, disturbing the stillness of primordial being, propels us

through the gates of death to experience (in rare cases) visions of different qualities of light that lead to liberation from duality or (more normally) visions that attract us back to duality, according to our habits and predilections. We choose what we can, depending on our fiber. But as the masters who claim to have seen the *bardo* states and rebirths clearly enough to remember them say, the condition of our minds in that bodiless period is one of extreme sensitivity: we have no solid husk to enclose our raw emotional nakedness; we are clairvoyant, volatile, and vulnerable; we feel the suffering we have caused; our joys and sorrows are exaggerated almost unbearably. Buddhism attempts to make clear the continuous sweep through lives, deaths, and rebirths of this mind-entity and why its restless activity provokes many incarnations, until liberation is achieved and the karma is finally dissolved into "one mind."

Music is a kind of practice for death. Although that may sound morbid to us, in a Buddhist perspective "death" is just a keener exposure to the problems of the lives both preceding and to follow, so it is entirely relevant to life now. Stockhausen put it like this: "Has it been stressed enough that the kind of music and the amount of music one has heard during one's lifetime is decisive for the soul's state and decisions after death?"[14]

This is one of the great mysteries of music: it leads right into the meaning of death. Death, the modern taboo, together with its concomitant, "consciousness," is the great enigma we all, however "scientific" or positivist we may be, are obliged sooner or later to confront. No one has explained it (the rationalist says). Though perhaps an explanation has been with us all along, but we were not aware of it: the experience of music.

The extreme mind experience of the *"bardo* of becoming," as it is called, does seem close to what music is about—raw, partially disembodied feeling-flow, relating to our underlying unity. Music differs from life as postmortem life differs from earthly life. Like experiences of life after death, music is clearly illusion, a "form of emptiness." Music is not *really* frightening, angry, joyful, or anything else; nevertheless, we readily construct thought-forms and give them reality as projections onto the sounds, remaining all the while more or less conscious of the elaborate artifice in which we are engaged. One of the disciplines of Tibetan monks is to construct beautiful mandalas of sand, over several weeks. When completed, the colorful faces, bodies, animals, and so on portrayed in the mandala are swept up and thrown into the river to be washed away into some other form. Like the forms of the sand, nothing exists from its *own side*, during life, after death, anywhere. Even we ourselves do not have inherent existence. We and the world are more or less shifting, fleeting rearrangements of "dry sand" scooped into shapes and named for convenience of reference. As with sand, so with sound. Ambiguity, being several things at once, is everywhere. All five hundred middle Cs in a symphony are different, yet, equally, they are all the same. The same cells are likewise different each separate time they occur, whether in the guise of tune, accompaniment, or contrasting tune. Any note can at one and the same time be part of a rising line and a falling line (see example 35).

Notes belong to several keys simultaneously, depending on your level of listening. They are at once part of a fused blend and an individual line. Lulu's murder is made of the same elements as Sarastro's pronouncement of enlightenment. The most contrasted tragedy and comedy are but temporary fixtures, violently real, but not so.

As with sound, so with all existence. Everything has parts, and the parts have parts, in an infinite regression, yet the sum of the parts is not the same as the whole. The whole cannot be found; nor can the parts. This is "emptiness."

I am not my body. I am not my mind. I am not the whole collection of my body and my mind, since the parts do not make a new whole, except for convenience of reference. Neither am I outside my body and mind as some "soul." Me and my other do not exist from their own side except by conventional imputation. They cannot be found. All turbulence, all suffering, arises from erroneously imputing real (as opposed to conventional) existence to "I" and to "the other." When this is deeply understood—and that is normally thought to take years of practice—compassion is felt. *Seeing through* suffering, *seeing through* our unliberated state of *samsara,* as an ignorant and tragically unnecessary condition for living beings, is "compassionate wisdom." *Music is a picture of "wisdom."* That is why music of suffering is often, paradoxically, so beautiful, so touching—even uplifting, inspiring.

Who then, in the last analysis, *is* the composer? The composer has no *inherent* existence. All one can say is that the "composer" is focused toward wisdom, inseparable from the universe: the universe is expressing *itself.*

Notes

Preface

1. Jamie James, *The Music of the Spheres: Music, Science, and the Natural Order of the Universe* (New York: Copernicus, 1993), p. 241.

Chapter 1

1. F. X. Witt, quoted in Karl Gustav Fellerer, *Mozarts Kirchenmusik* (Salzburg: L. Schaffler, 1955), p. 11. (Stravinsky agreed with this judgment, except that he enjoyed the "immoralities"!)

2. Hans Kung, *Mozart: Traces of Transcendence* (London: SCM Press, 1992), p. 69 (including Barth quotation).

3. Raymond Warren, speech at a congregation of the Senate and Council of Bristol University, conferring an honorary degree (1994).

4. Louis Spohr, *Autobiography* (New York: Da Capo Press, 1969), 2:57.

5. Igor Stravinsky, *An Autobiography* (London: Calder & Boyars, 1975), p. 53.

6. Otto Deutsch, *Schubert: A Documentary Biography*, trans. Erich Blom (London: J. M. Dent, 1946), p. 337.

7. Franz Liszt, "Berlioz and His 'Harold' Symphony" (1855), in *Source Readings in Music History*, ed. Oliver Strunk (London: Faber, 1981), 5:110, 113.

8. *Revue S.I.M.*, March 15, 1912; quoted and translated by Marc Pincherle in *Musical Creation* (Washington, D.C.: Library of Congress, 1961).

9. Arnold Schoenberg, "The Relation to the Text," in *Style and Idea: Selected Writings of Arnold Schoenberg*, ed. Leonard Stein, trans. Leo Black (London: Faber, 1975), p. 142.

10. Karlheinz Stockhausen, *Towards a Cosmic Music*, ed. and trans. Tim Nevill (Longmead, Dorset, Eng.: Element Books, 1989), p. 4.

11. Ibid., p. 67.

Chapter 2

1. Albert Low, *The Wounded Surgeon*, unpublished manuscript.

2. Johann Wolfgang von Goethe, *Gedenkausgabe der Werke. Briefe und Gespräche* (Zurich, 1949), 16:199; quoted and translated by William Pastille in "Music and Morphology: Goethe's Influence on Schenker's Thought," in *Schenker Studies*, ed. Hedi Siegel (Cambridge University Press, 1990), p. 32.

3. Heinrich Schenker, *Das Meisterwerk in der Musik: Ein Jahrbuch* (Hildesheim: G. Olms, 1974), 2:41; quoted in Pastille, "Music and Morphology," p. 37.

4. Igor Stravinsky, *Poetics of Music in the Form of Six Lessons* (Cambridge, Mass.: Harvard University Press, 1942), p. 140.

5. Beethoven, *Briefe und Gespräche*, ed. M. Hürlimann (Zurich: Atlantis Verlag, 1946), p. 146. Bettina's report to Goethe, which she assured him, on the strength of her excellent memory, was very nearly verbatim, is quoted by Susanne Langer in *Feeling and Form* (London: Routledge & Kegan Paul, 1953), p. 131.

6. David Bohm, *Wholeness and the Implicate Order* (London: Routledge & Kegan Paul, 1980).

7. Hans Keller, *Essays on Music*, ed. Christopher Wintle (Cambridge: Cambridge University Press, 1994), p. 198.

8. Letter to George and Tom Keats, December 21–27, 1817, in *Letters of John Keats*, ed. Robert Gittings (Oxford: Oxford University Press, 1970), p. 43.

9. Conversation between Debussy and E. Guirard, October 1898, taken down by Maurice Emmanuel (in Debussy exhibition, Paris, 1962).

10. Gustav Mahler, letter to Anna Bahr-Mildenburg, July 18, 1896, in *Alma Mahler, Gustav Mahler. Briefe* (Vienna: Zsolnay, 1924), p. 162; translated by Sam Morgenstern in *Composers on Music: An Anthology of Composers' Writings from Palestrina to Copland* (New York: Pantheon Books, 1956), p. 312.

11. Low, *Wounded Surgeon*, chap. 1.

12. John Rahn, "Differences," *Perspectives of New Music* 31, no. 2 (1993): 66.

13. Julian Johnson, "The Subjects of Music: A Theoretical and Analytical Enquiry into the Construction of Subjectivity in the Musical Structuring of Time" (Ph.D. diss., University of Sussex, 1993).

14. Low, *Wounded Surgeon*.

15. Hegel, *Aesthetik* III.iii.2, quoted by Liszt in "Berlioz and His 'Harold' Symphony," p. 109.

16. Curt Sachs, *The Rise of Music in the Ancient World* (New York: W. W. Norton, 1943).

17. St. John of the Cross, *Living Flame of Love*, trans. E. Allison Peers (London: Burns & Oates, 1977), p. 18.

18. Refer to the experience recounted by Paramhansa Yogananda in *Autobiography of a Yogi* (London: Rider, 1950), p. 128.

19. Julia Kristeva, "Revolution in Poetic Language," in *A Kristeva Reader*, trans. Toril Moi (Oxford: Basil Blackwell, 1986), p. 97.

20. Richard Wagner, "Beethoven," in *Richard Wagner's Prose Works*, trans. W. A. Ellis (London: K. Paul, Trench, Trubner, 1895), 5:75.

21. A similar discussion of spectralism will appear in a forthcoming issue of *Contemporary Music Review*.

Chapter 3

1. George Steiner, *Real Presences: Is There Anything in What We Say?* (London: Faber 1989), p. 232
2. Ibid., p. 196.
3. Rahn, "Differences," p. 67.
4. Low, *Wounded Surgeon*.
5. Ferrucio Busoni, *Sketch of a New Esthetic of Music* (New York: Dover, 1962), p. 85.
6. Liszt, "Berlioz and His 'Harold' Symphony," p. 114.
7. W. B.Yeats, *Essays and Introductions* (London: Macmillan, 1961), p. 67.
8. Oliver Sacks, *Awakenings* (London: Picador, 1973), pp. 283, 294.
9. Richard Tarnas, *The Passion of the Western Mind* (New York: Ballantine Books, 1991), p. 428.
10. Some of what follows is adapted from my article "The Metaphysics of Live Electronic Music," *Contemporary Music Review* 18, part 3, pp. 79–82.
11. Recorded by Tagore's friend C. F. Andrews in Tagore Rabindranath, *Letters to a Friend,* ed. and with an introduction by C. F. Andrews (London: Allen & Unwin, 1928); quoted in F. C. Happold, *Mysticism* (Harmondsworth, Middlesex, Eng.: Penguin Books, 1963), p. 140.

Chapter 4

1. T. J.Diffey, "Art and the Transcendent," *British Journal of Aesthetics* 34, no. 4 (1994).
2. William James, *The Varieties of Religious Experience* (London: Longman, Green, 1919).
3. For a clear discussion of vertical time, see Jonathan D. Kramer, *The Time of Music: New Meanings, New Temporalities, New Listening Strategies* (New York: Schirmer Books; London: Collier Macmillan, 1988).

4. R. Rangaramanuja Ayyangar, "History of South Indian (Carnatic) Music from Vedic Times to the Present" (Madras, 1972), p. 11; cited in Bonnie C. Wade, *Music in India* (New York: Prentice-Hall, 1979), p. 13.

5. See, for instance, Robert Sherlaw Johnson, *Messiaen* (Berkeley: University of California Press, 1975); or Paul Griffiths, *Olivier Messiaen and the Music of Time* (London: Faber & Faber, 1985).

6. Letter of Webern to Hildegaard Jone, January 16, 1940, quoted in Hans Moldenhauer, *Anton von Webern: A Chronicle of His Life and Work* (London: V. Gollancz, 1978), p. 566.

7. See, for instance, Webern's letter to Schoenberg of January 13, 1913, quoted in Moldenhauer, *Anton von Webern*, p. 126.

8. Toru Takemitsu, *Confronting Silence: Selected Writings*, trans. and ed. Yoshiko Kakudo and Glenn Glasow (Berkeley, Calif.: Fallen Leaf Press, 1995), pp. 51–52.

9. Joscelyn Godwin, ed., *Music, Mysticism, and Magic: A Sourcebook* (London: Routledge & Kegan Paul, 1986).

10. Rudolf Steiner, *The Inner Nature of Music and the Experience of Tone*, trans. Maria St. Goar, ed. Alice Wulsin (Spring Valley, N.Y.: Anthroposophic Press, 1983), p. 15.

11. Ludwig Wittgenstein, *Lectures and Conversations on Aesthetics, Psychology, and Religious Belief*, ed. Cyril Barrett (Oxford: Basil Blackwell, 1966), p. 23.

12. See, for instance, Daniel C. Dennett, "Are Dreams Experiences?" in *Brainstorms: Philosophical Essays on Mind and Psychology* (Montgomery, Vt.: Bradford Books, 1978); and T. C. Moody, "Conversations with Zombies," *Journal of Consciousness Studies* 1, no. 2 (1994).

13. The importance of this word is convincingly supported by the philosopher Renee Weber in her book on scientific and spiritual unity. She writes: "All mystics agree that language and schema attempt in vain to translate that ineffable domain into our feeble symbols. They are all shadows on the wall in Plato's cave, though to different degrees. Eckhart in fact places the reality behind the shadows quite beyond verbal reach, saying

'There is nothing in all the universe so much like God as silence.' Even so cautious a characterization as 'the unconditioned' can only approximate to the reality to which it refers. Therefore all schemas, words, concepts, formulae and formulations, whether scientific or mystical, suffer from the flaws of the Cave. These designations have a relative reality and a relative usefulness, but mystics caution against taking them too literally and against confusing the names with the reality. Hence Eckhart's earnest prayer of protection from this fallacy: 'I pray to God to keep me from "God."' Granting this limitation of language, the one word repeatedly used by mystics to describe their experience is 'unity'" (Renee Weber, ed., *Dialogues with Scientists and Sages: The Search for Unity* [London: Routledge & Kegan Paul, 1986], p. 7).

14. Stockhausen, *Towards a Cosmic Music,* p. 137.

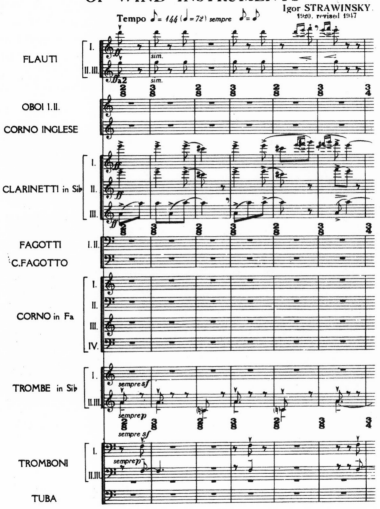

Example 1.   Stravinsky, *Symphonies of Wind Instruments*

Example 2

Example 3

Example 4.   Mozart, Piano Concert in C Minor, K. 491

Example 4, continued

Example 4, continued

Example 4, continued

Example 5.   J. S. Bach, *St. Matthew Passion,* "Am Abend da es kühle war"

Example 6.   Stravinsky, *The Rake's Progress*

Example 7. Stravinsky, *The Rake's Progress*

Example 7, continued

Andante Comodo

Example 8

Example 9.   Mahler, Symphony no. 9, first movement

Horn

Example 10.   Mahler, Symphony no. 9, first movement

I.

Example 11.   Mahler, Symphony no. 9, first movement

Example 12

Example 13.   Beethoven, Symphony no. 3, first movement

Example 13, continued

Example 13, continued

Example 14

Example 15.   Mahler, Symphony no. 9, first movement

Example 15, continued

Example 15, continued

Example 16. Wagner, *Götterdämmerung,* act 3

Example 17.   Mahler, Symphony no. 9, first movement

Example 17, continued

Example 17, continued

Example 17, continued

Example 17, continued

Example 17, continued

Example 18

Example 19

Example 20.   Wagner, *Parsifal*

Example 20, continued

Example 20, continued

leaves. ASCHENBACH follows them down the Merceria.
Familie verlässt die Kirche. ASCHENBACH *folgt ihr die Merceria hinunter.*

Example 21.   Britten, *Death in Venice*, act 2

⊕ At these points each solo voice should enter in canon when the previous voice has reached 𝄉. The speed should start
strictly, but in the *crescendo* should become faster and freer.

⊕ *An diesen Stellen setze jede der Solostimmen im Kanon ein, wenn die vorangehende 𝄉 erreicht hat. Das Zeitmass soll
streng beginnen, aber im Crescendo immer schneller und freier werden.*

Example 21, continued

Example 21, continued

ASCHENBACH suddenly comes face to face with the family. He
Plötzlich steht ASCHENBACH der Familie gegenüber. Er ver-

bows, raises his hat and turns away.
beugt sich, zieht seinen Hut und kehrt sich ab.

Example 21, continued

Example 22. Richard Strauss, *Salome*

Example 22, continued

Example 22, continued

Example 23.   Brahms, *Ein Deutsches Requiem*

Example 23, continued

Example 23, continued

Example 23, continued

Example 24.   Pärt, *Passio Domini nostri secundum Iohannem*

Example 24, continued

Example 25.   Tavener, *Ikon of Light*

Example 26

Example 27.   Berg, Violin Concerto, second movement

Example 27, continued

Example 28. Fauré, *Requiem,* "In Paradisum"

Example 29

* Ces chiffres indiquent pour chaque durée sa valeur en triples croches.

Example 30.   Messiaen, *Livre d'orgue,* "Soixante-quatre durées"

Example 30, continued

I.KANTATE

für Sopran-Solo, gemischten Chor und Orchester

Worte von Hildegard Jone
English version by Eric Smith

1.

ANTON *WEBERN*, op. 29

Example 31.   Webern, First Cantata, first movement

Example 31, continued

Dein lie - bes

Example 32.   Webern, Three Orchestral Songs, "O sanftes Glühn der Berge"

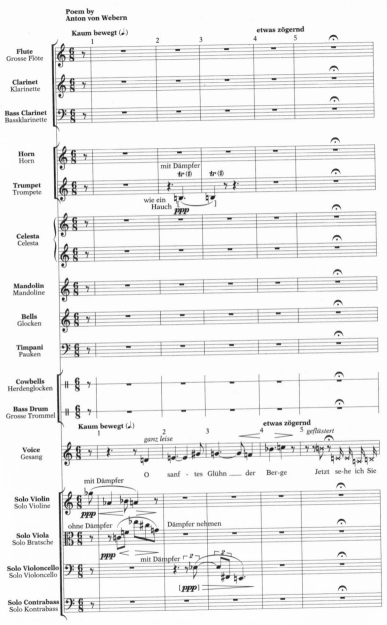

Example 33.   Webern, Three Orchestral Songs, "O sanftes Glühn der Berge"

Example 33, continued

Example 33, continued

Example 34.   Takemitsu, *Entre-temps*

Example 34, continued

Example 35

Index

Compositor: Braun-Brumfield, Inc.
Music setter: Ernie Mansfield
Text: 10/13 Aster
Display: Frutiger
Printer and Binder: Haddon Craftsmen